The Practical Preacher

The Practical Preacher

Handy Hints for Hesitant Homilists

Paul Edwards

Gracewing.

A Liturgical Press Book

The Liturgical Press
Collegeville Minnesota

First Published in 1994
Gracewing
Fowler Wright Books
Southern Avenue, Leominster
Herefordshire HR6 0QF

Published in the United States of America and Canada by
the Liturgical Press, Collegeville, Minnesota 56321.
ISBN 0-8146-2334-4

distributed

In New Zealand by	*In Australia by*
Catholic Supplies Ltd	Charles Paine Pty
80 Adelaide Rd	8 Ferris Street
Wellington	North Parramatta
New Zealand	NSW 2151 Australia

ISBN 0 85244 241 6

Typesetting by Action Typesetting Limited, Gloucester
Printed by Loader Jackson, Great Britain

Contents

Cyflwynir y gyfrol hon i
Yvonne Myra Davies
gyda diolch a chariad.

Foreword

Pope John said to a young man who longed to be a martyr, 'Be a teacher. It is much more difficult!' I think Pope John's advice could also refer to the preacher. Most clergy that I have met become reconciled to their duty of preaching to their people every Sunday, but few admit to being good at it. It is difficult to preach well and yet it is one of the most important and fruitful aspects of priestly ministry. Father Paul Edwards, S. J. knows all this and has written a book that is eminently practical, eminently readable and eminently useful. He is too modest when he claims that his purpose is to help the neo-ordinand to be competent in preaching. In my view, his book on preaching will be of enormous help to clergy who have been many years in the ministry and who need to reflect and renew in their own lives their ministry of preaching the Word of God.

The author directs retreats at St. Beuno's Spiritual Exercises Centre and there are many, including myself, who have profited from his wise direction. In writing this book, Fr. Edwards has drawn on his rich experience as a lecturer, a teacher, and a university chaplain. This book is not a narrow one because the factors in preaching which the author deals with, such as a sense of audience, dexterity with words, and flexibility of voice, are relevant to every occasion when one is asked to say a few words. Here is practical help at its very best. I have rarely read a book which gives such encouragement, not only to the incipient preacher, but to those of us who have been trying to improve the mastery of this art over very many years.

The book ends with Fr. Edwards' adaptation of the words of a friend whose disability called for 'courage, common sense and love'. This formula, he believes, applies also to other situations, including preaching. One needs courage to accept the responsibility of preaching. Of common sense you can never have enough as you decide on your material, your style, your exposition and your application. And if there is no love, leave the whole business alone.

May this book be a source of encouragement to all those who are called to preach the Good News of Jesus Christ in a manner that evokes a response of understanding and of faith.

Rt. Rev. Cormac Murphy-O'Connor
Bishop of Arundel and Brighton.

Acknowledgements

In presenting this volume to the public I wish to record my indebtedness:

to Mrs. Ruth McCurry of the religious publishing world who first suggested that I write on this subject and who assured me firmly that I was qualified to do so.

to Fr. Damian Jackson, Director of St. Beuno's Centre, who has always left me with sufficient free time in which to write.

to Fr. Anthony Nye who studied the text in detail and made a number of imaginative suggestions.

to Patric Byrne, deacon in the diocese of Wrexham, and Aled Jones, deacon in the Presbyterian Church of Wales, both of whom read the first version of the book and provided both encouragement and practical criticism.

to Miss Elizabeth Swayne who most generously volunteered for the laborious chore of correcting the proofs.

to Mrs. Sylvia Crozier for her typing, so efficiently and expeditiously done.

to the St. Beuno's Community who have patiently tolerated the taciturnity and despondency which a sustained effort at writing always engenders in me.

to Miss Yvonne Davies of the Clwyd Library Service. When unable to work because of a swiftly degenerating heart-lung condition and subsequently during her long convalescence from a double lung transplant, Yvonne checked every word of each version of this book, always doing so both promptly and meticulously. To her this book is gratefully dedicated.

Introduction

Discussing the structure of a sermon, I say in Chapter 7 of this book, 'I often find the introduction quite hard'. A few sentences further on I speak of 'the time and trouble which an introduction may cost me'. Faced here with the more complex problem of introducing, not a homily, but a book about the preparation and delivery of sermons, I have adopted the simple and economical tactic of explaining my choice of title, 'The Practical Preacher'. So:

The Practical Preacher

The adjective in my title has, I believe, a three-fold justification; for, as I hope to show, the work has a practical origin, a severely practical purpose and a thoroughly practical foundation.

Origin

'You do everything at St Beuno's to train people to give retreats except help them to give homilies'. In that remark lies the genesis of this book. It was made to me one rain-sodden summer by a young Scots nun who was working with me on a retreat. She was referring to the practice followed here, and at many other retreat houses, that during a retreat all directors, ordained and not ordained, take their turn at 'saying a few words' about one of the readings of the day. Many of the unordained even, to my surprise, experienced lecturers and ex-head teachers, find this a quite frightening ordeal. My

1

Scots colleague was a shrewd, streetwise, highly qualified social worker, quite accustomed to standing in full view of a large congregation translating the service into sign language. Nevertheless, up to that point she had always avoided by one stratagem or another giving one of these homilies. On this particular retreat there were only three directors and her sense of team loyalty won the day. So, grasping as it were both the nettle and the lectern, she successfully delivered her first, and in the course of the same retreat, her second homily. She also registered the above comment.

Impressed by this perfectly valid criticism, I pondered her words for the rest of the year. The eventual result, after some experimentation, was a quartet of optional half-hour talks which I used to offer during our three months course on Apostolic Spirituality. I also volunteered to help anyone on the course to prepare and deliver their first homily if they wished to clear that particular fence during their sojourn at St Beuno's. This offer was often accepted, and it was from that particular mustard seed that this book has grown.

Purpose

Part of that development has been a shift of focus. My four talks were aimed primarily at helping unordained retreat directors with their retreat homilies. In this book my primary concern has been to give practical, down to earth help to ordinands faced with the work of preaching. Most of the services which they will take are going to include at some point 'the sermon' or 'the address' or 'a homily'. I have aimed in these pages to help the neo-ordinand acquit him/herself competently in that context. If their seniors can find anything here which will help them in any way to scrutinise their performance, reassess their methods of preparation or in any way augment their effectiveness, that will be an added bonus.

Foundation

When it was first suggested that I develop my small scale effort on behalf of the retreat director into a full book on the preacher's craft, I demurred. When the only result of my disclaimer was to have the suggestion reaffirmed in stronger terms, I felt obliged to weigh the matter more carefully. Remembering Luke's advice to the man who dreamed of building a tower, I conducted a survey of my assets to see if they could be made to stretch to the realisation of this particular project. First of all I reviewed my own experience of preaching.

My first pastoral experience after ordination was as an assistant chaplain on an American Air Force base in Oxfordshire. There for fifteen months I preached every Sunday to American servicemen and their families, the Stars And Stripes hanging beside the altar. The long years since have heard me preach in all manner of parish churches, rural, inner city and suburban. I preached Sunday by Sunday during my three years in the Bristol University Chaplaincy, and then two or three times a term in the Leeds Chaplaincy over a period of six years. After that came another six years, this time in Oxford, whose Chaplaincy heard my voice on many occasions. I have also over the years preached in a number of schools, to innumerable religious communities, in Anglican Churches and Free Church chapels, in several Oxford colleges and a number of times in Oxford Prison.

It is not irrelevant, I reflected, as I continued with my audit, that I have also given many a 'preached' retreat, days of recollection galore, several courses of lectures and a host of talks on quite diverse subjects to even more diverse audiences. I am not here confusing lecturing with preaching. The material, the audiences, the whole ambience are quite different. On the other hand, a lecturer has to select his or her material, shape both it and the style of presentation to the occasion and the audience, and finally deliver it orally face to face. These are techniques which a preacher needs, albeit working with different material and in quite a different mode. These techniques of selection, adaptation and oral delivery are also required, but with different material again and in more demanding circumstances, from the schoolteacher. I was a classroom teacher for twenty-three years. I have therefore been well placed to reflect upon both the overlap and the differences between classroom teaching, lecturing, public speaking and preaching. Public speaking has crept into that list because for thirteen years I coached Sixth Form boys and for two interesting years boys and girls together, in the fundamentals of public speaking. In addition, I have as I have already described, tackled the problem of helping the adult give his or her first homily. As for the media, I judged that my television appearances have been too short and my radio broadcasts too few to be brought into the reckoning.

My stocktaking had turned up rather more in the way of resources than I had anticipated. Enough there for a tower? All that preaching, teaching, lecturing, coaching has not built me into a star preacher, still less an expert on the theory of Homiletics. However it does I decided, add up to a sizeable mass of relevant experience which analysed, reflected upon, organised and competently written up, should provide some worthwhile building material. Enough perhaps to raise a modest but serviceable tower. A watchtower, you will remember (Isaiah 5.5: Matt 21.33), was a feature of any well equipped vineyard. I have tried to provide a tower from which the apprentice vinedresser may survey the preacher's section of the vineyard, get his or her bearings and perhaps feel a little bit more secure in face of the future.

When I began work on this book I assembled and started to dip into a collection of other people's writings on this subject. I soon stopped. I decided that I would offer to the ordinand only the distillation of my own working experience, together with the results of my Christmas Card Enquiry (see Chapter 1). The only authority I quote is the Second Vatican Council whose relevant pronouncements I did re-read. I had to steep myself in them two decades ago when I wrote a small work on 'The Theology Of The Priesthood'.

If the purpose of this book is 'severely practical' and its material restricted to my own experience and the yield from my Christmas Enquiry, it is not I promise you a narrow treatment of the subject. I am careful to place preaching among other forms of public speaking. I insist that such factors as a sense of audience, dexterity with words and flexibility of voice are relevant throughout every aspect of pastoral work from the full dress sermon to the telephone conversation. I also believe that a novice lecturer and anyone whose work or spare time activities requires them to address an audience or merely on occasion 'to say a few words', could find help in these pages ... practical help! Perhaps they would be well advised to skip the earlier sections of Chapter 1 and begin with the part 'A Medium You Can Master'. They should find it heartening.

1

Practical Prerequisites (1) Confidence

A Christmas Surprise

One Christmas all my friends got a surprise. When they opened my Christmas card there fell out of it a sheet entitled 'Better Preaching'. It informed them that I had been asked to write a book about preaching and was now appealing for their help. 'I am asking you as a New Year's present to write to me about the preaching you hear and how it might be improved'. To spur their reflections I provided some headings:

> Subject and Treatment,
> Expression – Verbal and Oral,
> Manner,
> Stance and Movement,
> Preparation,
> Length.

'Draw on your Christmas goodwill and New Year freshness', I concluded, 'and write to me'.

Almost everyone replied. Most of them had obviously taken a good deal of trouble. One friend wrote early in February, 'I have not been idle all the time, for I have been trying to get the measure of feeling across the age groups in the parish'. Some of my contacts got together to frame their answers. Others enlisted the help of a prayer group to produce a collective response. A few made copies of my enquiry and persuaded friends and colleagues to send their own sets of answers. Some of the most painstaking contributions came from people I had never met. There were letters which covered three or four large sheets of paper with pertinent observations concisely stated.

Many of my friends are teachers in universities or schools, so their comments were based on their own experience of instructing, explaining and persuading. The members of the medical profession gave my questions the careful, detailed study which they obviously give their patients. The engineers were methodical and very definite in their opinions. Some of the responses were from Anglicans and some from members of the Free Churches. The majority, however, came from Roman Catholics. Clearly, my friends do not constitute a sociologist's sample of all British churchgoers. They have nevertheless provided me with a collection of real value on which I shall draw throughout the course of this book.

To my relief my enquiry did not release a flood of dissatisfaction. There were only two sweeping indictments, the more pithy of which described the local preaching as 'unfortunately audible'. On the other hand, of the two most detailed studies one started off, 'I ought to begin by saying how much I think the standard has improved in general', and the other ended, 'I feel that in general the faithful are lucky to have such skilful exponents to bring home the message of the gospel'. Most replies expressed satisfaction with some aspects of current preaching and a strong wish for improvement in others. Their criticisms were sometimes tempered with the sympathetic realisation that for the parochial clergy preaching is just one demanding duty among so many. Predictably, no preacher on earth could satisfy all my respondents simultaneously. Some of them expect an address to take at most seven minutes; others feel slighted by anything under a quarter of an hour. Some people want a preacher to draw on his or her own experience, while others find this approach quite distasteful.

A Medium of Some Importance

Yet, no matter how contradictory their views, no matter how divergent their advice, on one fundamental point there was no disagreement whatsoever. Preaching is an important matter for all of them. No-one dissented. An ex-headmaster, who now has great difficulty in controlling his pen, making an heroic effort, completed my enquiry and finished, 'After the celebration of the Mass there is nothing more important than the preaching of the gospel'. Others made the point that the Sunday sermon is for so many people the sole medium of instruction. Even where there were no such explicit statements, the care that had obviously gone into framing the replies and the degree of feeling coming through them was a convincing testimony to the importance people attach to the quality of the preaching they hear. Reading and re-reading their replies, I am very grateful that in preparing each sermon or homily, I have usually spent on it all the time and energy I had available.

At this point my mind goes back to an incident in a Jesuit refectory some thirty years ago. In the course of a meal I happened to remark, 'After all, I was ordained to preach'. At the head of the table the Rector looked dubious. He chewed on my remark briefly, then shook his head dismissively. 'No you weren't. Not to preach. You were ordained to offer sacrifice'. The Rector was not dogmatising on his own account, but stating a view which dominated our theology of the priesthood for centuries and can be traced back as far as St Jerome. This theory focused exclusively on the Christian presbyter as standing in the line of Melchisedek and Aaron, rather than as participating in the complete Apostolic mission to 'make disciples of all nations . . . teaching them to observe all I have commanded you'. (Matt. 28)

The Second Vatican Council was to adopt a very different perspective. In the 'Dogmatic Constitution of the Church', the Council defined the presbyterate, not in terms of any one function, but in its entire relationship with the episcopate. Priests, it says are 'helpers' of the bishops and therefore 'teachers of doctrine, priests of sacred worship and officers of good order' (Section 20). The clearest statement comes in Section 28: 'By the power of the Sacrament of Orders . . . they are consecrated to preach the gospel, shepherd the faithful and celebrate the divine worship'. The same doctrine is taught in three other decrees of the Council ('The Bishop's

Pastoral Office', The Ministry and Life of Priests' and 'On Priestly Formation'). It was gratifying to have the Council fill my hand with trump cards, even if it was a decade too late to play them at that particular table.

The theological theorists responsible for my Rector's dictum had dissected the presbyteral mission into different functions, and then fastened on one, the offering of sacrifice, which they declared to be the essential element, thus downgrading the others. The Second Vatican Council achieved a richer vision by presenting the different priestly activities as aspects of a single priestly mission, as facets of an organic whole. The Mass itself, on which the sacerdotalists so rigidly focused, testifies to the greater wisdom of the Council's approach. From the beginning the Christian liturgy has combined the Sacrament of the Body and Blood of Christ with the proclamation and explanation of the word of God. The two are knitted together in a single act of worship as the different acts of a play are fused into a single drama. The presentation of the word of God in the Foremass prepares us for the re-presentation of the Word in the Eucharist. The proclamation of the word achieves its consummation in the Consecration and then in Communion. In less technical language, the word comes to our ears to be received into our minds and hearts and so prepares us for Christ the Word who comes to us in Communion.

In the local chapel (Presbyterian) where our ecumenical service is held every third year, the pulpit could hardly be more conspicuous. At the east end of the building is a platform (Y Set Fawr) where we ministers sit. In the centre of the platform is a dais, which in its turn serves as a base for the all-dominating pulpit. There the preacher is elevated far above the rest of us. In the village church, a pre-Reformation edifice, the pulpit stands to one side over against the north wall. Here at St Beuno's there is no pulpit at all. There is no pulpit, as there is no baptismal font, because we are not a parish church. Of course, people have preached here for almost a century and a half, but they have done so without a pulpit. Admittedly I am forcing things a bit, but for me the relative position of the pulpit in these three buildings corresponds to the importance attached to the work of preaching in the three traditions. In the Free Church tradition the sermon is of overwhelming importance. Among Anglicans it has a well established, if less preponderant place. Among British Catholics its importance has sometimes been allowed to dwindle almost to a vanishing point.

I doubt if there has been in my life-time a single Catholic priest in Britain who explicitly thought of preaching as unimportant. However, many of them behaved as though it were, because other obligations bulked larger or seemed more urgent. A priest's first duty was to supply the Sacraments, to say Mass, to hear confessions, to take the Last Sacraments to the dying, to baptise and to marry. Then there was parish visiting, and the administration of the parish, the schools, the parish clubs. So preaching often became a Cinderella given nothing like the care and attention owed to her. The neglect was in no way wilful. Her noble lineage was never denied, but she seldom went to the ball, except during the parish 'mission', when she really came into her own.

That situation belongs I hope to the past. Which is not to say that it is now irrelevant. We start where our past leaves us, and our British Catholic past has not left us with a robust sense of the importance of our preaching either in theological theory or pastoral practice. Consequently, I believe the first need of a fledgling Catholic preacher is to have a lively conviction that preaching is a really important activity.

Some twenty years ago I was preparing a small work on the Theology Of The Priesthood. An important part of my preparation involved seeking out and weighing carefully every reference to the priest and his functions in the documents of the Second Vatican Council. There I found that the Council consistently places the 'ministry of the word' on the same lofty plane as general pastoral care and leadership in worship, frequently mentioning it first. In preparation for this book I read with equal care through the written views of my friends and my friends' friends, and from their comments learned how much our preaching, and the quality of that preaching, matters to them. So, the episcopate sitting in the solemnest form of conclave declares our preaching to be of the first order of importance, and the laity from their lowly benches, drawing not on abstract theological principles, but on their week to week experience, say the same thing. It is for us, sitting at our desks, preparing our addresses, and later standing in the pulpit or at the lectern, to attune first our minds, and then our performance to the expectations of both Council and congregation.

The majority of churchgoers do not attend Bible study groups, take part in shared prayer sessions or go to 'Talks On The Faith'. Would that they did. They very much need to have their Christian Faith explained in adult terms, to be encouraged to express that Faith in their daily conduct and, perhaps the most urgent need of all, to be given the inspiration to do so. Where will this be done, when will this be done other than in your Sunday address? This puts a great, perhaps intolerable, weight on the preacher, especially where people demand that he or she accomplish all this in no more than seven minutes. What are you to do?

I once read of a criminally neglected child who, when 'taken into care', could not be got to eat anything except crisp crackers. The matron, drawing on her inventiveness and her knowledge of dietetics, concocted a series of pastes which, spread on the crackers, saved the child from the worst forms of malnutrition. I conceive of the Sunday sermon as rather like that life-saving paste. We might wish that people were absorbing religious knowledge and inspiration more often and in a variety of forms, but in the circumstances it is up to us to serve all the nutrients we can by this one means, while keeping it acceptable and digestible.

You undoubtedly think of the ministry as important or you would not be offering yourself for ordination. You probably attach at least a moderate degree of importance to preaching. Should you at any time waver on the point I suggest you ask yourself three questions:

> Who am I, when I am preaching?
> Where am I when preaching?
> What am I trying to do when I am preaching?

To take the first point: I preach as an accredited representative of the Church which commissioned me to preach. If when I preach what I say is shallow and unhelpful, if it is poorly planned and badly phrased, the examples confusing and the applications I make ludicrously unpractical, what is the effect? Not only do I look incompetent, but because I represent the Church, the impression can be given that the Church has nothing worthwhile to say on this subject, or perhaps any other; that its teaching is irrelevant to people's lives, that religious thinking is shallow and confused and that the Church is an ineffectual, bumbling institution.

Of course it is illogical for people to project onto the whole Church the inadequacies of a single individual, but there are few persons completely immune from the emotional, if not entirely rational, impulse so to react. It is my responsibility to see that this situation does not arise. I must never give anyone the slightest inducement to think along those lines. Rather, I must bring my congregation something of the wisdom of the Church, its long experience of human beings, its care for them and − very important − my deep personal respect for the people in front of me.

Where am I when I preach? Answer: 'In Church'. This does not necessarily mean that I am in an ecclesiastical building. It may be a scout camp, the school gym or the cinema of a USAF base. I am 'in church' nonetheless because I am leading God's people gathered for formal worship. If I am preaching at the Eucharist, I shall be re-enacting the Last Supper with them. The sermon must be worthy of the occasion. I am not saying that it should be solemn, but that it should be a thing of quality. The thinking in it should be perfectly sound to reflect the deep truth of the ritual. The construction should be firm and the phrasing competent, to match the careful structure of the service and the dignity of the prayers.

What am I trying to do when I preach? My answer would be that I am working 'to continue the Incarnation'. Christ revealed God by living a human life, by his human actions and in human words. He used images conceived by his human imagination and phrases selected by his human intellect to appeal to the minds and hearts of his fellow human beings. This revelation the Church must re-express and transmit to succeeding generations, so that each generation should receive it into their minds and hearts and lives, and then re-express it for the generation that follows. As a minister of the

Gospel I have been appointed to this work of first receiving Christ's revelation into my own heart and mind and life, and then communicating it to the minds and hearts of my congregation, so that it may be re-expressed in their lives. In this way the Incarnation, the expression of the Divine through the human life of Christ is in some degree re-articulated in human life after human life. My preaching should be a deliberate, conscious and conscientious effort to sustain that saving, transforming process.

A Medium of Some Impact

I have just looked up the world 'sermon' in the 'Oxford Thesaurus' and read through its list of synonyms: 'lecture, lesson, preaching, reprimand, reproach, reproof, remonstration, remonstrance, scolding, harangue'. It gets worse as it goes along, does it not? With that cluster of associations working against you, your belief that your preaching matters will need to be clearly thought out and strongly held. It will have to cope with a number of discouraging reflections, not just a propos your own talents, but, more insidiously, as to the utility or futility of your even trying. People may say, 'What is the point? Nobody listens to sermons', or 'Preaching is an outmoded form of communication'.

I sympathise with this last allegation. In my first year as a teacher I could spend forty minutes in the bottom stream hammering away at French grammar. It was an inept thing to do, but I confess that in my inexperience I did it. I managed this with no other aids than the blackboard and the class textbook. In my last year in the schoolroom I found it harder to get the top stream to concentrate on a well produced video, than it had once been to make the lowest stream bend their minds to the textbook. 'Chalk and talk' have long been out, but when I preach I do not even have any chalk. How can you hope to hold with only your naked voice people used to watching expertly produced entertainment on television and able to turn from channel to channel as the whim takes them? The strange thing is that it can be done, and in fact is being done on a regular basis. I have seen in the eighties university halls crammed for some attractive visiting lecturer. There are speeches at party conferences and trade union congresses which are obviously being listened to . In the United States, with the most 'entertained' people in the world, there are evangelists – not Catholics or Episcopalians, I admit – who build auditoria to hold the thousands whom their preaching draws and holds. There is still an advantage in the directness, the immediacy of a speaker's presence and of his or her voice and personality. It attracts, but it is only an initial advantage, and you must exploit it quickly, using your voice and presence to good effect.

It is not true people don't listen. I have usually found that people will listen if you have taken the trouble to prepare something for them and are plainly making an effort to reach them. I once experienced the contrary. I was a visiting preacher at a Corpus Christi celebration. The Church was full; the congregation obviously devout, and feeling more confident than usual I cheerfully launched my prepared address like a newly completed ship down the slipway . . . and it sank like a block of stone. My schoolmaster's antennae were receiving a single, constant message, 'No-one is listening'. The congregation did not fidget; they sat in devout submission as though I were reading some long Latin formula which they could not follow, but which they believed to be an important part of the ritual. It was an unnerving experience. I dutifully projected my phrases one after the other into the air where they seemed to die somewhere above the congregation's heads. The congregation with a matching conscientiousness sat patiently on. It was horrible.

The next day I described my experience to a fellow teacher who lived in the parish. 'We don't listen', he said, 'One priest is quite inaudible. You can hear the other alright, but you can't distinguish a word'. That occasion is deeply scored in my mind because it is so abnormal. I am far from claiming that every congregation I have ever addressed has hung on my every word. However, I do believe that I know whether the general atmosphere in a church is one of attention or inattention, and I maintain that if one tries to give people something worth listening to, and tries equally hard to make it easy for them to listen and to hear, they will normally respond with their attention. That Corpus Christi celebration is an authentic example of the exception proving the rule. In their replies to my Christmas enquiry three of my lay colleagues quoted sermons of mine. The most recent sermon was delivered in March 1974, another in 1973 and the earliest about 1960. People do listen and some even remember. They may even be influenced!

My mother spent part of her old age in an Old People's Home run by the 'Little Sisters'. To be near her I once spent a month there acting as relief chaplain. When the first Sunday came round I learned that in the evening there was to be a 'Sermon And Benediction'. This was unwelcome news. I was unwilling to preach. Many of the old folks were deaf, and I saw no sign of hearing aids. Most of them looked as though they needed every bit of their physical and mental energy just to get them through the day. They should not, I thought, be expected to concentrate on a sermon. And who was I, priest or not, to be thrusting spiritual counsel on people at the end of their days, of whose special needs I had no experience? Of course, I kept my reluctance to myself, and preached. To have departed from the routines of the house would have caused consternation, speculation and even distress. I took for my subject that least practised of Christian virtues: forgiveness. I had prepared carefully; I spoke slowly and clearly; the old people watched me respectfully and I took it for granted that for all their polite attention my words would pass them by as transitory as the rumbling traffic outside.

Next day I had lunch with my mother as usual. In the middle of the meal she remarked, 'One of the old ladies came up to me this morning. I hadn't spoken to her before. She said "After listening to Father last night I have decided to forgive my sister"'. With that incident my respect for the medium of preaching rose like a lift going to the top floor. It was not my eloquence, for that had been deliberately subdued; it was certainly not my personality, as that also had been muted for the occasion. It was the clear statement of the gospel message in an ecclesial context that had proved so effective. Preaching is important, is appreciated and can be surprisingly effective. The surprise is often the preacher's own.

A Medium You Can Master

Preaching is, I readily admit, a formidable business. As a preacher I am answerable to the Lord of the Gospel, to the Church which commissioned me, and the people I serve. I am accountable for the accuracy of my message, for its relevance to the life of my congregation and for the effectiveness of my delivery. I need to be theologically competent, pastorally aware and verbally and vocally adequate. In fact if you were to draw up your own list of the various aspects of preaching and the qualities required under each aspect, you might well despair of being halfway fit to enter a pulpit. Please do not let this book have that effect upon you. You know that soldiers say, 'Time spent on reconnaissance is seldom wasted'. Read this book as a form of reconnaissance. It should help you to focus more accurately on the different facets of preaching and then to seeing your way to tackling and mastering them.

Preaching requires guts. Have the guts to preach even though you know you do it imperfectly. Have the gumption to face those defects and work at them despite the fact that you are unlikely to turn into another John the Baptist or John Chrysostom. Don't let yourself off with such evasions as 'It is not really my thing' or 'You have to have a gift for it'. You were not born walking. You had to learn, clutching at people and furniture. You almost certainly had some disconcerting tumbles, but they did not in the end prevent you from learning to walk and even to run. When you preach there will be nobody to clutch at, so do not be surprised if at first you proceed rather unsteadily. Should you have the misfortune to stumble quite nastily, do not despair. Give yourself time; pick yourself up; learn from experience, and with the brave persistence of an infant, try again. Remember at the same time that there is no paragon (a perfect diamond weighing at least 100 carats) of a preacher ready to step into your black shoes and preach in your place.

'You have to have a gift for it'. That misleading comment contains two pernicious fallacies, as we shall see.

Towards the end of my last year as a teacher I was invited to the Sixth Form Leavers Dinner. As we were assembling in the dining-room the boy organiser came over to me and spoke the dinner-ruining formula, 'You will say a few words at the end of dinner, Father'. I took my place at table scrabbling in my pockets for a scrap of paper on which to make notes and a biro or pencil with which to write. I had changed into my best suit and had none of these things! Throughout the dinner I laboured frenziedly at trying to put a speech together. My neighbour did not get a word from me other than a muttered apology for my not being able to talk. When food was put in front of me I swallowed it hastily, tasting nothing as I continued to rack my brains for something to say. By the time the dinner drew to a close I had strung a few thoughts together, found a few phrases and with a borrowed biro had jotted down about eight key words on the back of my inch-wide place card. It was an easy audience to address, the boys euphoric at having left school, the teachers gratified to be welcome guests and no longer class enemies, so my improvised speech went down quite well.

Next morning in school a kindly young teacher came up to me and said earnestly and wistfully, 'I did envy you last night. You have a great gift'. I hope he received a gracious reply because, although I appreciated the compliment, its wording exasperated me. Had he envied me sitting through a dinner I did not taste, a pleasant relaxed occasion turned for me into one of strenuous, nervous, mental and imaginative effort against the clock? Did he envy me the succession of practice sermons as a student, most of them bringing on nervous diarrhoea beforehand? Did he envy me the scores of times that I had stood in sacristies dismally convinced that the sermon on which I had spent so much time was certain to be a failure? 'A great gift'! Behind that evening's performance lay my experience as a boy debater, years of sermon practices at the seminary, twenty-five years of preaching, twenty-three years of teaching, numberless addresses to various groups on a variety of topics and all the previous occasions when I had been asked to 'say a few words'. A gift? Those 'few words' of the previous night had been very dearly bought.

I have told this story because the word 'gift' is far too glibly used. It usually ignores the great importance of training and the indispensibility of practice, experience and dedication. That is the lesser fallacy. The greater one is that it divides the human race into a small minority who have the 'gift' in question, and the general mass of people who, should they try to be musicians, artists, actors or orators, will only meet with failure.

The population is not divided into a very small group with intelligence and the rest of us who are totally unintelligent. There is a small percentage of highly intelligent people and an equally small group of very low intelligence. The rest of us lie somewhere along what the statisticians call 'the curve of normal distribution', some highish, an equal number lowish, with the largest numbers towards the middle. Why should it be different for any other factor? To make music, to decorate, to address a group and even, I suspect, to act, are basic human activities, and therefore the innate capacity for them is 'normally distributed'. It is certainly not a case of a small elite being given 'the gift' as though by a fairy godmother at their christening, while the rest of us have no potential whatever.

To realise their potential the very able and the less able alike require training and experience. They will also need 'teachability' a robust determination and a capacity for sustained, painstaking effort. With those qualities and the right opportunities the very able may go on to achieve star rating, and a much larger group with less 'flair' acquire a solid competence. That at least is within the compass of the normal ordinand.

With persistence he or she may find that they have flair and can achieve distinction. I take it for granted that any ordinand is teachable, resolute and hardworking; that is part of their vocation.

After the formal presentation of my material in this first chapter I now offer the reader the following imaginary dialogue. It is meant to serve as something of a 'chaser' to Chapter 1 and perhaps as an aperitif to Chapter 2. It is lighthearted in tone and wholly serious in intent.

Extract from a tutorial on preaching

The Practical Preacher   Tell me! What do you believe to be the first needs of a preacher? If you yourself are to be a preacher what must you have?

Hesitant Homilist	Er ... A clear, flexible voice? ... Skill with words? ... A good presence and the ability to project oneself?
P.P.	Not bad! An interesting list. But those things are tools. Very good tools, mind you, but preaching does not start in the orator's toolbox. It begins in the mind and heart of the preacher. So go a little deeper. Try again.
H.H.	Err ... A lively faith? ... A sense of mission? ... A competent grasp of Theology?
P.P.	Again a very good list! All those things are necessary. But they are needed in every department of the ministry. They ought to be behind everything that you do, or try to do, for your people. Now, what of preaching? Specifically of preaching? What are the basic requirements there?

(H.H. frowns, stares at the P.P.'s feet and is silent.)

P.P.	I'll tell you. You must have Confidence and Passion. You need confidence in preaching as an important activity; confidence that preaching can be an effective medium, and, not least, confidence in your own capacity with training and experience to use that medium competently ... Passion we can discuss next week.

2

Practical Prerequisites (2) Passion, Respect And Disengagement

A Passionate Preacher

Do not be put off by the term 'passionate'. I am not going to suggest that you ought to preach with blazing eyes and frenzied gestures, your voice tense with urgency and your style one of unrelieved declamation. Heaven forbid!

Let me begin with that least fanatical of figures, the amusing after dinner speaker. Aware that he has been invited largely to entertain, his approach will be for the most part light-hearted and even at times frivolous. Nevertheless, as a real games player is always intent on winning, so a real speaker will always want the diners' full attention and will aim at it from start to finish. He will work, showing no signs of the effort, for the appropriate responses: laughter at his jokes; that touch of expectancy in the air as a story moves to its climax; a softening of mood should he become a little sentimental. He will woo the company, wanting them to warm to him, or rather to the persona he has decided to present to them. Behind a very relaxed exterior there will be an unwavering firmness of purpose to which I have given the label 'Passion'.

I used a slightly different term to Richard one morning in 196–. Richard, the Captain of our debating team, was the most gifted boy speaker I was ever to coach. His predecessor as Captain had been a shrewder debater and his successor was to be a better political orator. Richard's advantage lay in his greater literary skill and his considerable charm. At his best, the gleam was not so much in his eye as in his whole delivery.

That morning I did not know what to say to him. We were standing in our unlovely school canteen, all glass and grubby brick, rehearsing for a public speaking competition. Richard had composed a good speech. It was neatly on the subject; it ran gracefully and was witty throughout. He was speaking at the right pace; he was making all the correct pauses; he was enunciating clearly and yet the whole performance was about as interesting as if he were slowly unwinding a ball of string. What was I to say or do? In the end the formula just burst from me ... 'Richard', I exclaimed, 'a speech is a love affair with the audience!'.

Never a lad to be caught without an answer, Richard drew himself up, assumed an air of offended rectitude and said primly, 'Father, I am not that sort of boy'. That was persiflage. He had grasped at once what I was looking for, and our rehearsals took off immediately. On the night Richard was the last to speak, which is always a severe test of an entrant's nerve. Richard kept his. When his turn finally came the phrases flowed from him as from a well played harp, his stance was relaxed, modest and unassertively self-possessed. It was a performance which sparkled throughout and the audience loved it.

Richard left with the first prize and I came away with a problem. Just what had I meant by that formula which Richard had understood so promptly and which had so thoroughly transformed his performance? Could I make the same point in other terms with someone less literary, less intuitive? I used the term 'passion' above to describe that fixity of purpose and the vigilant determination which lies beneath the apparently casual approach of the good after dinner speaker. Below I offer the following analysis to cover both phrases.

When you address an audience:

you must want the attention of that audience;
you must want their whole attention and you must want it badly;

you must want to move them, to lead their minds and feelings in a certain direction, so that for the moment it is the most important thing in the world that you succeed.

This does not call for either volume or vehemence. It is a matter of intensity. When I was a nine-year old, I and the other lads from our street got a lot of fun from playing with a magnifying glass. We would use it to concentrate the sun's rays − on those days when the sun co-operated − and so set a light to bits of paper which we found in the gutter or took out of dustbins. When I spoke of 'a love affair' to Richard, and when I talked above of 'passion', I was asking for that same intensity of focus and for a similar concentration of mind and will. When you are speaking it should seem as though there is nobody else in the world but you and those you are addressing; nothing of any consequence in the world other than your winning their acceptance for what you are saying. For the time being the world has shrunk to this audience, the things you want to say to them and yourself saying them.

I do not apologise for putting the preaching of the Gospel alongside, though not among, wholly secular forms of public speaking. The minister of the gospel needs to be − God help us all − a teacher, a counsellor, a public performer, an organiser and a leader. In all these activities he or she is a human being dealing with other human beings by human means. The same factors are at work as when other human beings are counselling, teaching, etc. Of course, there must be a spiritual dimension to all our work and we should never lose sight of it. Yet that spiritual factor does not lift us clear out of the human world in which the Word became incarnate and of which He was a living, speaking, active, suffering part.

This evening I took six forms of public speaking and asked myself where each overlapped with the activity of preaching. I passed in review:

the lightweight after dinner speech,
the opening address at a conference,
the 'few words' of the distinguished old boy at the school prize-giving,

a trade union official appealing for 'industrial action',
a politician soliciting votes and
a lawyer winding up his or her case.

Like the preacher all six want the ATTENTION of the audience, and if they are doing their job seriously, its complete attention.

Then they all want to MOVE the audience in some way, to produce an atmosphere, to form an attitude among their hearers or to coax them to act in a certain way. The after dinner speaker wants the diners to feel relaxed and entertained. The prize-giving guest is expected to speak appreciatively of the school, and, if he can rise to it, offer a word of edification to the usually unimpressed pupils; the welcoming speaker at the conference aims to pull together a host of individual participants in the cheerful anticipation of furthering their common interest. The union official, the politician and the lawyer have the more urgent objective of a vote, a verdict.

Finally, and this came as a surprise when it dawned on me, all six classes of speaker could be described as 'MINISTERS'. Each of them is, at least in theory, working for the benefit of others. They all speak to serve, as it were; the post-prandial orator for the diversion of the diners; the prize-giver to further the purpose of the school; the opening speaker to get the conference off to a good start; the union official for the benefit of his members; the lawyer on behalf of his client; the politician for his party. I was also intrigued to realise that each speaker had been 'MISSIONED', the after dinner speaker and the conference opener by the appropriate committees, the prize-giver by the school authorities, the official by the union and the politician by the party. The lawyer represents a client, but also has a general licence to plead from the Law Society or the Bar Council.

I have analysed the overlap between preaching and the other forms of public speaking, not for the intellectual satisfaction of seeing how far I could push a formula, but to make a very practical point. Because of that overlap a preacher should always be ready to learn from those who practise other forms of public speaking. If I want to know about catechetics or counselling, then I must read and listen to secular educationalists and psychologists. In the same way, if I wish to be able to address a congregation competently and effectively, I must be open to absorb all I can from those who speak effectively to rather different audiences in quite another context.

With Respect, Sir ...

A week ago I walked into our dining-room and asked, 'Which is more important, to love people or to respect them?' My colleagues obviously wanted to answer 'to love', but glimpsing the problem hesitated. One tried to side-step the dilemma, 'Surely, if you love somebody you respect them'. 'Not necessarily', I countered. I had been turning the matter over in my mind for some hours and had considered that possibility. 'You can love somebody and believe that you know what is best for them, so that you override their views, leaving them no freedom of choice. Then you are respecting neither their judgement nor their right to assume responsibility for their own lives'. We left the matter open.

And content I am to leave it, so long as we aim at both, a love with respect. I incline to think that we should make sure of respect first. We should be very careful that we both think of and behave to a congregation with a really adequate respect. It is not something that we can take for granted. Those who 'minister', e.g. clerics, nurses, teachers, have the relevant knowledge, the training, the experience and the responsibility. They are therefore in a superior position, and from a superior position it is easy to look down and to be patronising. Most professionals manage to overcome this temptation rather better, I fear, than many a priest. In the Catholic Church we are not helped by the title 'Father' with its regrettable implication that we are dealing with children. Also, we act and speak in the name of a Church which has become highly centralised, unrelievedly clerical in government and is not in the habit of wielding authority with a light touch. During my seminary years we often heard the phrase, 'the simple faithful'. (The most cynical of my fellow students remarked, 'Were the faithful ever that simple ... or that full of faith?') The phrase was useful in so far as it reminded us that in our ministry we would need to break away from the technicalities and intellectual subtleties of our Theology course. The snag was that 'simple faithful' were thought to need 'good simple piety', which was too often an excuse to serve up a thin gruel of religious platitudes, 'simple' only in the sense that there was nothing much to it, and 'good' for very little.

I should respect the individuals in a congregation because they are human beings made in the image of the Divine, with intelligence to understand, minds to appreciate and hearts to love. I must respect them as Christians called to know and follow Christ. I should reverence them as a group because they constitute a Christian assembly, gathered to further their relationship with God through Christ. I should respect their many achievements, their knowledge, their experience of life, their skills, their many virtues. How much a congregation could teach me in how many fields and about how many aspects of life! Of the people in my congregation some will already be better Christians than I, and all of them are capable of growth towards Christ. How far that growth might take them, it is not for me to say. It is for me to play my modest part in their development conscientiously and respectfully.

Respect, rather like justice, should be there to be seen. Out of respect for my congregation, out of respect for the Gospel which I am handling and out of respect for this formal Christian assembly, when I preach my stance should never be slovenly, my diction slipshod, my material shallow or unsound, or my expression of it less than competent. My explanations should never sound condescending; the overall impression ought to be that I am offering people something, not thrusting it upon them. People should feel that I have taken trouble in my preparation for their sake and that I am making a similar effort in my presentation. They should feel that while I am preaching the whole of me is theirs.

Let His People Go

'They should feel ... that the whole of me is theirs'. A few paragraphs back I said, 'you must want the attention of that audience, their whole attention'. It is this total mutual absorption of speaker and audience, initiated by the self-giving of the speaker and reciprocated by the audience at which the 'real' or dedicated speaker aims. 'To want their attention, their whole attention ...' Does that sound like flagrant egotism? I can assure you that the vocation of a preacher leads in the very opposite direction. As a preacher it is important that one does not repel a congregation; and it will help if they like you. After that we are there to offer a message, a message which it is for us to deliver, but which is not ours in origin. The message is from God, in the first place, delivered through Christ. I am like a telephone engineer, important while the line is being installed, and once the line is in good working order, ready to pick up my tools and go.

The 'total, mutual absorption of speaker and audience ...' Does that sound as though the speaker were deliberately erecting a snug hothouse warmed by the mutual admiration of speaker and hearers? The vocation of the preacher calls for the very opposite. We are there to help people think in terms of the infinite and the eternal, to be vividly conscious of a world of grace and evil, of great suffering and everlasting good. That vision, even half communicated, is not at all cosy, and certainly reduces the preacher to scale.

The true preacher is like a signpost drawing people's attention, so that once they have absorbed its message, they can pass on beyond it. For me the model preacher in this respect is John the Baptist. John seems to me to have been the most effective preacher in the whole Jewish-Christian tradition. Jesus and Paul travelled to meet their audiences and sometimes sought out ready-made congregations in the synagogues. John installed himself 'in the wilderness' a thousand feet beneath sea level, where the crowds sought him out, disregarding the long, steep haul back to the uplands of Judaea or the mountains of Galilee. He worked no cures, performed no miracles and still they came. Some attached themselves to him as disciples, and the gospel bears witness to their austerity, their devoutness and their loyalty. Two decades later in Pisidian Antioch, hundreds of miles from the Jordan, Paul will confidently invoke the witness of John. Later still, and even further west, he discovered at Ephesus a community who had been baptised 'into the baptism of John'.

Yet John appears to have done nothing to promote himself, nothing to make himself acceptable, sometimes adopting an abrasiveness which we would be unwise to imitate. When people came in droves and hung on his words, he directed their attention elsewhere, insisting on his own insignificance. He focused on their needs and the power of him 'who is mightier than I'. It was for him to bow out, 'he must increase and I must decrease'. Are you not put in mind of the Pauline teaching in Philippians, that 'Christ emptied himself'? John after his extraordinary success in drawing and gripping the crowds 'emptied himself' by deflecting their interest towards Christ. Then Herod and Herodias took his 'emptying' to its final stages.

The Christian preacher will work hard to 'win' people, but never to keep them. We offer them all the knowledge, understanding and guidance we can, not to make them dependent on us, but so that they can learn for themselves, see for themselves and wisely choose their own way. We 'win' them to send them by their own route to Someone Else. We spend our energies to dispossess ourselves of what that expenditure 'wins' for us. Christ redeemed the world by a process of 'emptying' himself. It is our vocation to work with Him to the same end, and by the same austere and richly fulfilling formula.

3

On The Subject Of Subjects

The first topic my questionnaire raised with my friends was their preachers' choice of subject. It was the obvious place to start. Until you have decided at least tentatively what your subject is to be, you cannot begin to think about developing, illustrating, introducing and concluding.

Often, thank goodness, the question of subject is settled for you. There may be a major feast which is not to be ignored. It may be a wedding or a funeral or the celebration of some jubilee at which you are to preach, in which case the event dictates your theme. Outside the special occasion it is often taken for granted that you will comment on one of the liturgical readings of the day, usually the gospel. You have still to decide what you are going to say about those texts or the special event or the feast, but you have one less decision — often the most difficult — to make.

Most of my informants were quite satisfied that the preaching they hear should take its theme from the liturgy of the day. A few thought otherwise. They point out that for the majority of the congregation the Sunday sermon is the only instruction they ever get. The preacher should therefore cover the whole range of Christian doctrine, dogmatic and moral together with the application of Christian inspiration to contemporary social and political and even medico-ethical problems. He should also explain and uphold traditional devotional practices. None of my contacts put the point, or draw the conclusions quite as uncompromisingly as I have done here, but this position is the unexpressed basis of what several of them said. They have, you must admit, a perfectly logical case. But is it reasonable? Is it practical? Can, for instance, a priest giving a brief homily at the 9.30 Mass be expected to cover every aspect of the Christian life? Over how many years? At what depth? The demand is just not realistic.

Yet it should not be summarily dismissed. As pastors we need to be aware of all the needs of our people even though we can find no immediate practical way of meeting some of them. It is because we cannot cover in our routine preaching the whole of Christian doctrine that we need a sound system of priorities for selecting what we do deal with. We should know what topics we never touch upon, and be alert to the possibility of filling in some of the gaps on other occasions by some other means. So, while your choice should never be a matter of chance or whim, neither should it be rigid. Let it be adaptable in the face of experience, responsive to changing circumstances and open to the unexpected opportunity. In summary, select your themes deliberately, responsibly and flexibly.

Earthing The Gospel

For one thing all my informants seem to hunger, that their preachers should provide them with inspiration for their daily lives. In using the word 'hunger' I do not imply that they never get fed, or that they suffer from spiritual malnutrition, but that this need, like that of the body for food, is recurrent and exigent. One correspondent asks for 'preaching which allows the perspective of Kingdom values to address real human situations'. Says another, 'so often a subject seems far removed from daily life, an academic argument that may be far removed from our own worries and experiences'. A third, 'more emphasis is required on relating to the outside world and helping people to see where God *is* at work'. A fourth, 'preaching needs to be tied to the Scripture of the day, the current events in the world and the congregation's everyday experience'. Another, 'I believe people attending mass are looking for inspiration, something practical that they can do or carry out during the week ahead'. Each of these quotations comes from a different letter and were taken from among the first fifteen responses to arrive. I could fill a page with further versions from other letters of the same heartfelt plea.

A word of caution! One Good Friday, getting on for sixty years ago, my mother took me with her to church for the evening service. I think that we had already been to the Stations of the Cross in the afternoon. The evening service focused on the 'Mater Desolata', that is Mary as she is represented in Michelangelo's two Pietas, with the body of the Crucified in her lap. The preacher began with an eloquent exposition of the thoughts and feelings of a woman as she first takes her newborn child into her arms. He then drew a poignant contrast with the emotions of Mary on receiving the dead body of her son from the cross. It was quite impressive. As we left the church afterwards my mother looked down at me reflectively and said with the down-to-earth scepticism of the working class, 'I didn't feel anything like that when you were born. I just thought, "Will I be able to do for 'im?"'

That was my first lesson in sermon making, and the one, I think, which I have most taken to heart. If, as people wish, you are going to deal with 'real life situations', try to get it right. Speak from your own experience or get your information from a thoroughly reliable source. Had I to tackle the subject of 'Mater Desolata' and decided to talk about a mother's feelings, I should be very careful to consult a number of women first, and to make it clear that I had done so; e.g. 'Several women have remarked to me . . . One woman even said to me . . .' I once heard a most moving sermon from an Anglican woman on the theme of Mary in which she drew upon the birth and growth of her two sons, including her reaction when one of them was arrested at a demo. We were fascinated.

Even when you are drawing upon your own experience there can be snags. 'On the whole we don't warm to preachers who draw upon personal experience to illustrate their themes. Precisely because it is personal it can actually jar or confuse', writes a university lecturer. His views are echoed by another lecturer, 'Some priests insist on giving embarrassing personal revelations designed, I suppose, to show that they are just like us. This approach can be overdone'. On the other hand a woman writes, 'The preacher's lapses are always interesting, and I can learn a lot more from your failures that I can from your successes'. Where does that conflict of witnesses leave you? It leaves you where any investigation into the tastes and preferences of any varied group will land you, with the conclusion that you cannot satisfy all the people all the time ... Of this quandary one particularly gifted ex-pupil says, 'Therefore they (the preachers) should go ahead with what they think is right'. Yes, but let the word 'think' refer to the careful, responsible judgement based on a knowledge of the congregation, and not merely on your own inclination, prejudice or whim.

I myself have always used situations I have been in, situations I have observed and situations described to me by others. I have done so because I wholly agree that the Gospel should be preached as having its application to every context in the life of every Christian. The Gospel is not so preached when we leave it 'unearthed'. The best schoolmaster I ever worked with comments in this context, 'I analysed a sermon I heard recently (analysed it on the hoof) and noted abstract noun piled on abstract noun urging us to practise charity. There was not one example of how, in our parish, we might do so'. That in my book is not preaching. It is talking about charity, though somewhat pointlessly; it is making a speech about charity, though certainly not a good one. Whatever it is, it is not preaching.

Remembering as I do my mother's deflation of the Mater Dolorosa address, my conviction that the Gospel must be 'earthed' is an uncomfortable one to hold. The typical congregation is lay, for the most part married with children and drawing its living from commerce, industry or administration. I am a celibate cleric who has spent his life in schools, seminaries and universities. How can I out of that restricted and very untypical experience 'earth' the gospel for the ordinary congregation? I have for the most part to draw on experience outside my own. I watch, I listen, I read and take my examples from what I have seen, heard and read. More importantly, I ask. I try never to press beyond the evidence (it helps to have read history). I hope that I never say, 'A mother always feels ...', but, 'Several women have told me that a mother ...' or 'X says in her biography that ...', leaving it to the congregation to decide whether they agree with my witnesses or not.

Leaving it to the congregation is something that I am increasingly prepared to do. As a young teacher I met schoolmasters whose ideal it was — very patchily realised — to make everything so clear that the pupils were compelled to understand. They would provide them with all the necessary information, with mnemonics to retain it and rules of thumb to make its application painless, and then give them plenty of examination practice. It was years before I realised that this was not to educate, but to drill, that it was a process of pre-digestion and spoonfeeding in which the pupils' minds were understretched and given little stimulus to grow.

Christ in the Gospels does precisely the opposite. He invites people to follow him, but never compels them. He offers whole areas of his teaching for people to ponder on and apply to their own lives, but allows them, albeit to their great loss, to leave his sayings unexplored. Some of the parables such as that of the buried treasure, or of the pearl of great price, consist of a single sentence. Our Lord does not tell the shepherd, the fisherman, the peasant, the household servant what assets they must be willing to liquidate in order to buy a field, or in exactly what coinage they are to pay for the precious pearl.

I used to blame myself that I could not speak to a congregation in terms of the factory floor, the office and the details of domestic life. Now I see my obligation to be to persuade them to do the work of translating the Gospel into the language of their own lives, to put it into the context of their own circumstances. It is my business to emphasise that this ought to be done, to convince them that it is worth doing, but not to do it for them. I try to give examples of it being done; I may offer suggestions, but to do it for them, or rather to attempt to do it for them, I would judge to be an impertinence.

Social and Political Issues

One topic I should like to leave alone, but in conscience dare not, namely the application of the Gospel to social and political issues. Earth the Gospel in that soil and you stand to get quite a shock from the resistant ground. Abstain from doing so, and you preach a mutilated gospel. Social and political factors are part of what a deeply reflective respondent termed 'the seamless robe of our lives'. Some of my replies complain that their preachers avoid this whole area, whilst another charges the local clergy with 'delivering political broadcasts with the Word as a veneer'. In this area you are very unlikely to please all the people all the time. We are allowed in this country to attack Communism and Apartheid, to neither of which ideologies our British Sunday congregations are likely to be tempted. Move nearer home, and you will soon encounter division and resistance.

This is territory where you must study the map, reconnoitre carefully and still walk warily. You need to ponder the general relationship of Christian ideals to social and political questions and then to have studied the individual issue. Your resulting comments must be well thought out and sensitively phrased. 'Is that not equally true', you might ask, 'whenever we preach, no matter what the subject?' It is true, but not equally true. There is a fluidity about social and political situations and an emotional volatility when they are being discussed, which are rarely present in other contexts. If your subject is the Incarnation or the Eucharist you do not these days run much risk of dividing and alienating. Speak pointedly on a social or political issue and you are only too likely to generate disagreement and antagonism.

Some of us timidly avoid such matters; others of a more combative personality may welcome confrontation, relishing, as it were, the brave clang of the gauntlet flung from the pulpit onto the flags of the central aisle. Both groups, it seems to me, are being self-indulgent. One does not have the courage to risk unpopularity; the other practically courts it, seeing themselves in an heroic pose. But there are other ways of challenging people to respond to the gospel besides accusing and denouncing them. People who have voluntarily come to church to worship have a sincere, if sometimes lukewarm and somewhat patchy, wish to be a good Christian. It is our business to build on the goodwill that is there, to help people to see the further implications of what they already accept in principle. It is for us to offer them the inspiration to give their Christian beliefs concrete realisation in the social and political sphere as well as in their private lives. We should persuade and convince, rather than denounce and berate.

I cannot deny that the Baptist, Christ and St Paul could wield their tongues like machetes. Our Lord chops the Pharisees up very small indeed. I should not advise that prophetic, charismatic stance. Charisms are given from above, not deliberately adopted. You would do better to model yourself on Paul writing his honeyed words to Philemon, on Christ dealing with the rich young man, or on John counselling the soldiers. When people ask 'What shall we do?', you have got it right. You are unlikely to bring a modern British congregation to that point by vituperation or nagging.

To Make Sense of The Gospel

Once when I was giving a very short course on the rudiments of preaching, an experienced priest, who paid me the compliment of attending each talk, took me by surprise with the question, 'What is your aim in a homily?' With no time to reflect I came back with the answer, 'To make sense of the gospel'. I was thinking of the address at Sunday Mass, the principal form of preaching among Roman Catholics and the extract from the evangelist read that Sunday (hence 'gospel' with a lower case 'g').

I went on to 'unpack' the phrase 'make sense' giving it four levels of interpretation:

1.   To explain the terminology and background
2.   To make the scene 'real'
3.   To extract the message
4.   To explore its relevance

Let us look at the four levels in more detail.

First, the terminology and background: I explain terms such as 'Korban', 'binding' and 'loosing' etc. I give whatever information is needed about the agricultural, political, social and religious background. Here I find myself having to comment on sheep rearing, to sort out Herod the Great from Herod Antipas, to cast some light on the feud with the Samaritans and the outlook of the Pharisees, and to give some notion of the layout of the Temple. I often find it desirable to comment on the Old Testament resonances behind the language of the Gospels. I try to make these explanations clear, if possible vivid, and which is the most difficult, short.

Secondly, to make the scene 'real': This second process, which may have been begun in the explanations of the first, can be the hardest part of the whole thing. Cecil B De Mille in his autobiography speaks of 'that stained-glass telescope which centuries of tradition and form have put between us and the men and women of flesh and blood who lived and wrote the Bible'. I am not sure about the word 'telescope'. True, it suggests distance, but a telescope brings things nearer while we practically put biblical characters on another planet. 'Stained-glass' I do like. The figures in a stained-glass window are immobile stereotypes in antique costume as cold and bloodless as the glass they inhabit. I have to get those people out of the stained-glass window and to make their characters, their experiences, their actions and words imaginable and credible. I have to turn them into human beings who were quite like ourselves but in different circumstances.

I remember one day flinching from commenting on the parable of the royal wedding in Matthew 22. The scenario sounds preposterous. The messengers who go out to summon the reluctant guests are physically abused by them and then murdered, which seems an exaggerated way of declining an invitation. The King reacts in the same dramatic fashion; 'he destroyed those murderers and burnt their city'. It looks as though Luke's (c.14) more credible story of the banquet and the unwilling invitees has become confused with the story of the vineyard and the violent refusal of the tenants to pay their dues (Matt. 21). I suggested the possibility of this confusion to the congregation. I also pointed out that the story makes a little more sense when one realises that a refusal to obey a royal summons to such a solemn occasion would be understood by both parties as a withdrawal of homage, an act of contemptuous defiance.

I then had the happy notion of asking a director of one of

Britain's largest industrial concerns what would be the position of a junior executive in a large firm who declined his invitation to the wedding of the Chairman's son and heir on the grounds that he was playing in a local golf tournament or redecorating his house. The answer came prompt and uncompromising. 'He would be finished in that firm'. Less drastic than having his house burned down, but one can see the same principle at work. That piece of information 'made more sense' of the parable for me, and I hope my congregation.

The third level of 'making sense' of a passage of Scripture, the one to which the first and second are quite subordinate, is to extract its message. The writers of the New Testament are never diarists or mere reporters. They are persistent teachers, one might even say propagandists. They have selected each piece of material, and shaped it to convey some truth about Christ, his life and his teaching. It is for the preacher, as the teacher of the congregation, to bring to the surface and to display as plainly as possible what it is the evangelist wants to teach. Sometimes the point is perfectly clear as in the parable of the lost sheep. Sometimes it has become tantalisingly obscure, as difficult to spot as a rugby ball in a fiercely contested maul; even worse, because in a rugby match there are only two sides, but in a good biblical ruck it is every exegete for his own theory.

I have recently read that which can be applied to the verse 'Do not hold me' (John 20.17) there are 'twelve different types of explanation'. How is the poor preacher to deal with this sort of situation? My own practice is to select one explanation and to present that, hedging it about with qualifying clauses such as 'these words may imply' or 'it has been suggested that' and the blessedly brief 'perhaps'. My sermon would have a much more authoritative ring to it without those qualifications, but my conscience insists on them. It forbids me to speak as though I am giving the one authentic interpretation of the text when there is no such thing. Nor will it permit me to ignore the commentaries and simply 'say what the passage means to me'. This is not a wholly illegitimate proceeding provided I make it clear that my interpretation is entirely personal and subjective, sparked off by my own reflections on the text. My objection is that it easily becomes a self-indulgent short cut substituting facile reactions for careful study.

Another text I do not like to see waiting for me in the Lectionary is Luke 14.26, 'If anyone comes to me and does not hate his own father and mother ...'. This is a fence I approach very carefully. To 'make sense of it' I start with the phrasing, suggesting that in the word 'hate' we have a Semitic idiom, a rhetorical device for emphasising a difference by exaggerating it greatly. I point out that Matthew's version (10.37) simply says, 'He who loves father or mother more than me ...'

To 'make it real' I try to show that in most cultures anyone's first loyalty is to family and kin. The family has given you life, reared you, protected you and provided a dependable support in an indifferent and often threatening world. You put the family first and they will always put you before anyone outside the family. I give examples of the corruption and injustice to which this clan loyalty can lead. Then, to show that this outlook is not limited to Asia and Africa I may quote the remark made about the Kennedy family in the days of J.F.K. and his brother Robert, that they judged every political event and situation in America or elsewhere purely in terms of its impact on the political standing and fortunes of the family. I may instance the example of a British multiple murderer who was twice given false alibis by members of his family, with the result that several more people lost their lives.

To 'extract the message' I point out that when a Jew or Pagan was drawn towards Christianity the greatest obstacle was often the breach with their family that this step would cause. The gospel writers, who must have watched that situation many times, want to emphasise that the pull of the family must not be the ultimate criterion. The following of Christ overrides all other priorities. Anything which blocks us from Christ is, in that respect and to that extent, a hostile and damaging force.

The fourth and final level at which I try to 'make sense' of any gospel reading is by insisting that its message is meant, in some form, to apply to us now. Here we are back with the job of 'earthing' revelation in the lives of the congregation, an objective already discussed earlier in the chapter.

Small Matter

There is one truth about the making of a sermon which I always point out to first time preachers, namely that they will require surprisingly little material. They seldom believe me. All first time speakers, not only preachers, nervously ask themselves, 'What am I going to say?' Fearful that they will run out of· matter, they pile up thoughts and reflections sufficient for a handful of lectures. Even a woman who had twice been a headmistress and had often addressed pupils and parents, persisted in the same mistake when it came to preparing her first 'short homily'. Her first draft included roughly twenty-four different reflections on the text. Unconvinced by my expostulation, but too polite to reject it outright, she cut them down to eighteen. The result was more like an overloaded lecture than a brief homily.

I should never go as far as those theorists who say that a sermon should have but a single point. That view I find too sweeping and too restrictive. However, it is true that one point effectively introduced, carefully explained and tellingly illustrated will provide a sermon of adequate length. Most first time preachers overestimate the amount of matter they need and then compound their error by seriously underestimating the length of time they will take to say it all. I have sometimes had the partly amusing, partly exasperating, experience of being told that the projected homily will take 'seven or eight minutes', when it had taken that long to read the plan to me. To the question of calculating the length of one's composition I shall return later.

Two Pleas

Among the comments about their preachers' choice of material sent by my correspondents two, I think, deserve special prominence. One was a complaint voiced in a group report about the regrettably common habit of preachers taking their congregation through the gospel story a second time, step by plodding step in their own uninspired and uninspiring words. The group described the practice as their 'pet hate'. An individual making the same point asked, 'Why put the message into a second-rate version when it is already written so much better?'

The other comment was in a different key. It came from an experienced nurse and health visitor and was at the top of her list of 'Subjects Neglected'. 'Failure, importance of, value of ... It's the heart of the gospel in a way. So many preachers make Christianity sound like a rat race to self-perfection, rather than a sharing in the Passion'. I hope that all those who read this book will become competent preachers, even distinguished ones. I hope that they will prove articulate, shrewd, clear, forceful, imaginative, transparently sincere, passionately concerned, inspiring but down to earth. Christ was all these things. Would you say, reviewing his life and work, that he was a successful preacher?

4

Ears Are Trumps

The staff of the secondary school in County Kildare raised an amused eyebrow each morning as they watched their new colleague, freshly hatched from the University, cross the schoolyard with bulging briefcase and an armful of books. They knew that the briefcase bulged, not with worksheets, but with her University notes, that the books were not children's books with large print and colourful illustrations, but austerely presented tomes of definitive scholarship. One of Ms Blue-Stocking's duties was to 'take poetry' in Class One. Class One was a likeable collection of twelve and eleven year olds, for whom most of the staff had a good deal of respect and affection, but of whom they unsentimentally remarked, 'They haven't got a brain between them'. It was to Class One that the Inspector went to observe Ms B-S 'taking poetry'. With awe and incredulity he watched her draw from her briefcase a lecture on Aristotle's 'Poetics', copied down in her student days, and read it unabridged and unexplained to a benumbed Class One. She must have read it at something of a lick, because she came to the end of the lecture with several minutes of class time still to run. The situation did not catch her unprepared. A second lecture was duly drawn from the rich word-hoard of her bag and the whole process calmly resumed. The Inspector's surprises were not yet over. Later in the day he interviewed the young woman and began to point out the deficiencies of her pedagogical approach only to run into total incomprehension. His observations meant as little to Ms B-S as Aristotle's 'Poetics' to Class One. He argued with her for an hour, wholly in vain. She took her stand on a

40

single issue. She went into the classroom with good material and plenty of it. To her that was the sole issue, and the only criterion of her teaching.

Her case is an extreme example of a very common disability which I call Novice's Myopia. It is a frequent reaction to the question, 'What am I going to say?'. This question all speakers, preachers, teachers and lecturers must put to themselves, the veterans as much as the novices. The difference between the veteran and the novice lies in the focus and the consequent response. The novice, unless very well trained, focuses on the 'What' and earnestly scrabbles around for material; good material and lots of it. The veteran extends the question to 'What am I going to say to this audience on this occasion?' and focuses on the audience and the occasion. The veteran is also in the market for good material, but by 'good' he or she means sound material which will prove nutritious and digestible to this audience. The material must be sound in itself. Unsound material, whether unsound theology or unsound literary criticism, will never be of any use to any audience on any occasion. If it survives this check, it must then pass the equally stringent but more subtle test of whether it will serve this audience.

I was preserved from the Irish lady's mistake by a kindly, if rough-handed, Providence, which, in the make-do atmosphere of 1946, dropped me into a classroom to teach thirteen and fourteen year olds French grammar and syntax. On the first day of school I was issued with three sets of textbooks, a very demanding one for the A classes, a less exacting one for the B stream and a more elementary one for the C stream. Streaming is now unfashionable, and perhaps rightly so, but that differentiation of textbook made it clear to me from the start that the same syllabus (all three streams were aiming at the School Certificate) must be presented at a different rate and at a different depth to different pupils. I conscientiously studied the books and, like the Irishwoman, sailed into my classes with my material at the ready. My Yorkshire pupils proceeded to teach me a much more valuable lesson than I ever taught them.

I learned very quickly that:

it is one thing to SAY something;
quite another to have it LISTENED TO;
a distinct third to have it UNDERSTOOD;
a different matter again for it to be REMEMBERED;
and a frequently unattainable fifth to have it PUT INTO
PRACTICE

Each stage of that quintuple process has to be fought, or less pugnaciously, worked for. To have secured one stage in no way guarantees that the next will follow. Nevertheless, the illusion that you have only to tell people something and that they will all listen, understand, remember and act on it, is a very obstinate one. It re-surfaces even among the experienced. A headmaster may lapse into saying, 'I told them about it at Assembly', as though the fact of his making an announcement guaranteed its absorption by the entire school. A parish priest can say indignantly, 'We informed them at Mass last Sunday' expecting the whole parish to have adjusted immediately to his new arrangements. Telling them is easy: it is the other four stages that will tax you.

I was also to learn that the achievement of each stage was not always easier in the better forms and predictably harder in the 'weaker'. I had more trouble getting a lively 4A to listen to me than the more stolid 4C, though of course when they listened 4A were quicker to understand. I also found that the more persevering members of 4B had better memories for the work than some of the more nonchalant pupils in 4A. That experience has its application to preaching. The more educated congregation is not always going to be the more receptive. Certainly they will be the quicker to grasp an explanation, but they may also be the quicker to switch off if they have decided you are not going to be very interesting. Because they read and discuss more, your words may have greater difficulty finding a niche in their memories than in those of a simpler congregation.

I also learned in school to take the day, the time, even the weather into consideration. You can tackle new material on a Monday which it would be unthinkable to introduce last period on a Friday. You can expect to get through more work on a fresh morning than in the late afternoon during a heat wave. You make better progress in the Autumn term than during the chill, weary, flu-ridden period between Christmas and Easter. A congregation, though less affected than a class of children is not untouched by variations of season and weather. A January morning, especially if the heating is on the blink, a sunny Spring evening, a stifling day in August (if there is one that year) all influence the mood, and therefore the receptivity, of the gathering. The same congregation in a different mood is not really the same congregation, and so requires for each change of circumstance an answering modification perhaps of matter, certainly of manner, in the preacher. Be brisk when the weather is cold: go slower, but quite firmly, when the weather is hot. Show sympathy if they have come through the drenching rain. Let them see that you inhabit the same world. In a word RESPOND!

I found Middle School French Grammar less than spellbinding. The school where I was trying to teach it stood near the centre of an industrial city. The air was laden with soot. When the wind blew from the wrong quarter it brought us the fumes from the local tannery, and the classroom reeked. From my own formroom I looked across a Lowry landscape of belching chimneys to Armley Gaol where hangings were still being carried out. In those unlovely circumstances I became a teaching addict. Marking was tedious at best and heartbreaking at worst; I left some classrooms frayed and frustrated; there was always that dismaying gap between what one wished to achieve and what one did achieve. And yet I was hooked. I was fascinated by the problem: 'I know this; I understand and appreciate this. How do I instil that knowledge, produce that comprehension, evoke at least something of my own appreciation in the minds of this class?' When I took leave of my last class hanging had long been abolished and the chimneys smoked no more. The public buildings had been scoured and their facades now gleamed white, as did my own hair. One thing had not changed. The fascination which the classroom and its multiple problems exercised over me was quite undimmed.

As a priest I am very glad to have served an apprenticeship in the classroom. A priest is a teacher when preaching, when presenting the liturgy, when instructing a convert, even when explaining something to a penitent. The classroom teacher's

mannerisms I try to avoid; a penitent does not want to be
addressed like a schoolboy, nor does the congregation at Mass
wish to be made to feel like the backrow of 4C. At the same
time I will do well to remember everything which my classes
taught me, the quintuple process of communication, which I
set out above, being an important example. Equally persuasive, perhaps even more radical, is what I would call the
Diarchy of the Sound and the Suitable. These two factors, the
Sound and the Suitable, are between them the absolute rulers
of every aspect of a piece of exposition. They exercise an
absolute veto. I must say only what is true; my every statement must be as accurate as I can in the circumstances make
it. That established, every choice I make – whether of
material, of level, of style, of vocabulary, of volume, of tone,
of stance, of length – must be made to suit this class/
audience/congregation on this occasion.

The Sound

You might think that the axiom, 'I must say only what is true'
is so patently true that it does not call for comment.
Regrettably, the matter is not that simple. No-one is going to
lie in the pulpit, but we can culpably mislead. We can do so,
I suggest, through lack of care, lack of qualification, and
through rhetorical and ideological self-indulgence.

Lack of care

To speak accurately about Scripture and Christian doctrine
calls for careful thought and a precise choice of words. Do I
always take that care? We can say, 'In this passage Our Lord
is saying . . .' and serve up a hasty, half-baked guess. I can
say, 'The Church teaches . . .', when it ought to be, 'I think I
remember my Theology textbook saying . . .'
    In the pursuit of accuracy we immediately run up against
the abiding and often acute problem of limited time and
perhaps limited energy. You will be a very fortunate preacher
if you can spend a large portion of the week in exegetical and
theological reading and reflection. You may have only the
minimum time for preparation, and perhaps lose even that

through some unforeseen caller or sudden emergency. What then? Honesty! 'Perhaps this parable means ...', 'I suggest Our Lord intends here ...' Such use of qualifying phrases, or, if you like, hedging, may go against the grain. You believe, quite rightly, that a minister of the Gospel should speak with the firm, clear ring of authority. So we should when we can; but to put forward the uncertain as certain, to dress up my own guesswork as though it were authoritative teaching is to mislead the congregation and to betray both their trust and that of the Church ... and all to save ecclesiastical face!

Lack of qualification

When, culpably or inculpably, our address is insufficiently prepared we will need to qualify some of our statements along the lines suggested. Often we do the very opposite. It is when I am underprepared that I am more likely to come out with sweeping assertions, to be overdogmatic and to sprinkle my sermon with 'every' and 'always' and 'never' when the complexity of the truth calls for a much more nuanced phraseology.

Rhetorical self-indulgence

This weakness also produces unjustified generalisations and misleading exaggerations. A speaker with a touch of oratory in his make-up soon becomes aware that it is comparatively easy to be eloquent when you are making universal assertions and issuing comprehensive condemnations, and quite hard to sound anything but flat and prosaic as you make qualifications and list conditions. Unfortunately for us would-be-orators truth is often complex, subtle and untidy and it is our business to 'tell it as it is'. The marriage of truth and eloquence calls for a skilful and patient matchmaker, and thereafter a competent marriage counseller to keep the partners together.

Ideological self-indulgence

This is my not altogether happy term for the practice of preachers riding their own religious hobbyhorse and airing their personal political and social views, presenting the whole package as so much Christian doctrine. The headmaster of a large comprehensive school complained in his letter, 'I recently heard a preacher tell people at mass that the Church required them to go to confession every three weeks, and it was as bald as that'. A consultant physician has a worse example, 'I once heard in all seriousness Dr Spock blamed for homosexuality and Aids'. He adds that he has often sat through sermons 'consisting of harping nostalgia'. An experienced priest certainly has the right, perhaps the duty, to offer practical pastoral advice to his parishioners and to commend such a practice as frequent confession. He is in the wrong if he attempts to swing the Church's entire teaching authority behind his personal, fallible judgement as to precisely how often his people should use the sacrament.

As for using preaching time to vent one's own dissatisfaction with our present world like some old club bore, and exploiting the ecclesiastical setting to invest one's petulance with an aura of religious authority, that is seriously wrong. Preaching is a sacred responsibility. The time and attention which a congregation is prepared to give us in the hope that we will lead them nearer to Christ, is also sacred. To use that function and their attention for my own gratification is worse than stealing the collection. It is the more serious misappropriation.

The Suitable

So fanatical have I become about the principle, 'every choice ... must be made to suit this congregation', that I now prepare a sermon with a mental image of the congregation in front of me. As I select my material, my examples, my words etc., I picture myself dealing with this subject, in that church, with those people. I imagine myself telling them that story, using those phrases. I am not claiming that this procedure guarantees the aptness of every choice. However I know that it helps. At Oxford when asked to preach in a college chapel I would go to the chapel the week before, although I usually knew it well, and stand in the exact spot from which I was going to speak. That way I could work on my address with a mental photograph of the setting. Once I was caught out. 'On the night, we filed into the Chapel and I saw to my consternation that the building was illuminated — which is stretching the word quite a bit — only by candles. My congregation were dim figures in the half gloom, their faces barely discernible in the dark spaces between the candleholders. Authentically mediaeval, of course, and romantic in a Pre-Raphaelite way, but very disconcerting to a preacher who likes to watch the expressions of his audience with the concentration of a marksman at Bunker Hill. 'Don't one of you fire till you can see the whites of their eyes!' Visualise your congregation beforehand, but never take it for granted that the situation will be precisely as you have foreseen. Do not feel aggrieved that things are not as you expected. The world is not under any obligation to conform to your predictions.

Suitable For Whom?

Three years after my ordination I was again appointed to teach, and flatteringly enough, at the same school where my services had been sought by the Headmaster. So I returned, contentedly enough, to the industrial smog and soot-blackened buildings of the West Riding. There I did my level best to communicate an enhanced sense of the Good, the True and even — Heaven help us — the Beautiful. That seemed to me less of a challenge than the one I experienced at the weekend in some local pulpit. My weekday classes were homogeneous. The boys in any one class were of the same age, had reached the same stage of intellectual development, and I knew just where they were in the syllabus. A Sunday congregation — and it was a different one each time — represented every decade of life and were drawn from a broad spectrum of education and occupation. I would look at them despairingly and think, 'At what level do I pitch this sermon (we did not yet call them homilies)?'

Thirty years later I still do not know of any simple way out of that particular impasse. No doubt a born orator, a saint or some charismatic evangelist would sweep them all off their feet, old and young, graduate and illiterate together. But what does your ordinary, conscientious, run-of-the-mill cleric do? Again, my personal solution comes from my experience in school. In the classroom I taught thirty-odd boys of the same age and standard, but the school assemblies were a different cup of tea. There I faced seven hundred of them from eleven year olds to the Upper Sixth with perhaps thirty members of the Staff present. 'Faced' is not quite accurate. The peculiar architecture of the school dictated that I stand at the side of the hall with five hundred boys turned towards me, and all the First and Second Form in the chapel behind me. Again the question: 'At whom am I aiming?'

My answer after months of experience: 'Do your damnedest to interest the Sixth Form and the Staff'. That answer was based on no elitist prejudice, but on sheer practical observation. I had simply noticed that if the Staff and the Sixth looked bored the rest of the school were not going to take an interest, and correspondingly that when the teachers and the Sixth Formers looked attentive there was quite a chance of my engaging the rest. I certainly did not neglect the others. I tried to keep the vocabulary and comparisons within reach of the younger; I was careful to throw my voice into every corner; I would rake the room from end to end with my eager gaze. I would swing half round from time to time to address the youngsters in the chapel directly. It was an energetic performance. An address of two or three minutes had to be carefully prepared and I used to pour myself into the delivery. It did the rest of my preaching a power of good.

I must emphasise that my aiming at the Staff and the Sixth Form was not exclusive. I held them, as it were, in the centre of my focus, and yet tried to keep everyone else within the field of my awareness and of my outreach. My approach to parish preaching developed along similar lines. My first objective became to provide solid mental fodder for the most thoughtful – not necessarily the most educated – and yet never to lose awareness of the rest of the congregation. I would always be trying to reach out to the latter, always trying to be aware of them in the pace and clarity of my explanation, in my choice of words and phrases. Whenever I heard myself come out with bookish phrase I would repeat myself using a simple, commoner vocabulary.

I am not claiming that I have found the only way to address the bafflingly broad mix of the parish congregation. I do think I have found one which works reasonably well. What I would wish to stress is the need that the whole congregation should feel that I have come with something to say, that I am trying my hardest to share it with them and to make it easy for them to understand and appreciate. At the same time one's energetic and eager performance should not sound coercive. I am offering something. I must offer it firmly, making the reasons for acceptance as clear and persuasive as I can, yet leaving the hearers their freedom. They should feel that they have chosen to accept what is being said, that they have judged it to be correct, not had it forced upon them. It seems to me that offering, not thrusting, leading and not compelling, is part of the respect owed to a congregation.

There are occasions when I completely reverse my method of tackling a mixed congregation. If there is a block of school children present I deliberately address myself to them. Over a year ago, on the Feast of the Assumption, there trooped into our retreat house chapel more than thirty Wolf Cubs with Cubmaster and Cubmistress. I sat the boys on the floor in front of the altar, and when I had read the gospel sat just in front of them on a low stool. I then asked the boys questions about the feast, gradually coaxing out of them its significance. The adults I did not even look at. A few months ago I met the Cubmaster and we reminisced about the occasion. He said with warm approval, 'You ignored the adults completely'. He was wrong. I knew that the adults would watch intently to see how that bookish priest would cope 'with those little boys', and that they would listen with fascination to the boys' replies, giving me and the boys a degree of attention that they would never have given me had I been addressing myself to them and not to the Cubs. You might say that I reached two audiences by concentrating on one. However, I warn anyone trying that formula for the first time, that one's questions to children have to be carefully chosen and carefully worded, and that a good deal of impromptu dexterity is needed in building on their answers. You can seldom anticipate what children will come out with.

The answers to my Christmas enquiry brought only one comment about the heterogeneous congregation. The writer was sympathetic, but critical:

'Now for content, and I feel myself in some difficulty here, for within the congregation is a wide variety of parishioners and the preacher must aim at the majority. In this they should be helped by the fact that the old ladies can be found at the early morning Mass, families at the 9.30 Mass, the more staid parishioners at what used to be the sung High Mass (11.00 am) and the young (or the young at heart) at the Folk Mass (6.00 pm). Where one of our priests has to say more than one Mass there will be no variation in the sermon regardless of the make up of the congregation'.

The writer seems to be more aware of the importance of 'suitability for this congregation' than the clergy are. Yet, as the same writer observes elsewhere, 'the clergy have to find time to prepare it (the sermon) within a very busy lifestyle'. Can they be expected to prepare more than one address for the same day? In theory the preacher could use more or less the same material at different masses with different illustrations and some changes of vocabulary. Yet even those variations will not prepare themselves.

The problem would be alleviated, I believe, if we thought consistently in terms of 'this congregation'. If we did so, some modifications would come almost spontaneously.

Were you to ask a good experienced teacher to address the First Form and the Sixth about the same subject in exactly the same way and in exactly the same words, I doubt if he or she could do it. They would automatically adapt their approach and their vocabulary to the class. Should the response of a pastor be any less sensitive? I may be asking too much. A teacher spends all day, five days a week teaching, whereas preaching is but one of a pastor's multiple activities. Nevertheless, we would do well to take the flexibility, the almost instinctive adaptation of the good teacher as our model. It is a rare priest, I hope, who would receive at the presbytery, a child, a teenager and a middle-aged adult, and address all three in exactly the same tone of voice with the same manner, using the same vocabulary. Can we not carry something of that instant responsiveness and that instinctive flexibility into the pulpit?

We certainly need flexibility when we meet a strange congregation. If invited to address a congregation hitherto unknown to me, I should pump the inviter for all the information I can get, and, time permitting, tap other sources too. Whether these enquiries yield a full and convincing description or a disappointingly skimpy one, I should arrive with my eyes skinned and antennae aquiver, taking nothing for granted. Does the appearance of the congregation fit the description I was given? Do they look like good listeners? Are they friendly from the start or do they need to be won? Do I need to be carefully formal throughout, or may I risk a more relaxed and intimate tone? Is my pace right? Are they still looking interested or should I take a short cut to the end? And so on.

The principle of 'Suitability For This Congregation' was impressed on us at the seminary. We knew the classic 'Punch' joke of the parson leaning out of the pulpit of the village church, beaming fatuously at a stolid, rustic congregation and saying archly, 'But I know what you will say to me. You will say to me "Sabellianism".' I also remember the cautionary tale of the Jesuit missioner, who addressing the congregation of a Lancashire mining town on the subject of Sunday Mass, declared in ringing tones, 'And when you go away for the weekend, always insist with your hostess that she make arrangements for you to get to Mass on the Sunday'. Sending you in the family brougham perhaps! I have often wondered whether the miners and their families, who at that period managed an occasional outing to Blackpool, were mildly gratified to be talked to as though they were gentry, and quite pleased to have the services, even temporarily, of a priest of such superior background. However, I doubt if there were any such considerations − or indeed much thought at all − in the mind of the reverend missioner.

On This Occasion

There was much less emphasis during our training on the other half of my phrase, i.e. 'on this occasion'. That phrase covers not only such events as weddings, funerals, first communions etc., but other less foreseeable circumstances. If the heating has broken down on the coldest Sunday of the year and the church is excruciatingly cold, your sermon, no matter how carefully prepared, will have to be sacrificed or at least drastically abridged. Excellent your homily may be, just like Miss Blue-Stocking's poetry lecture, but a congregation which is becoming chilled to the bone will be as unreceptive of its quality as those Irish First Formers, and much more resentful.

How obvious that is! Yet to many a speaker or preacher their prepared address is inviolable. Suggest that they do not give it, and they will look at you as though you were proposing to drown a child. Urge them to excise some section, and you will be made to feel that you are about to cut off one of their fingers. They have put work into this talk. They have decided on their subject, gathered their thoughts, planned the development, thought out some good illustrations with one or two telling phrases and are primed to deliver it. It is unthinkable that it should be suppressed or even seriously curtailed. Many years ago there was a famine in a rice growing area of the Indian subcontinent. Western relief agencies were quick to dispatch large shipments of wheat. The generosity and prompt efficiency of these organisations was much to their credit. Perhaps they were not to be blamed for not knowing that the stomachs of these lifelong rice eaters were incapable of assimilating wheat. A congregation may be incapable of digesting your grain, despite its quality, and not only when they are cold. They may be in a hurry as are the people at a lunch time mass who must still get a bite to eat and get back to work. They may be sated with words and ideas if it is an evening mass at a conference packed with talks and discussions. Insist on serving your own particular consignment of grain to people in these situations and they will become heartily sick of you.

In 1979 a mission in Rhodesia/Zimbabwe was attacked by guerillas. Two lay brothers were shot, but the resident priest, who had a gun of his own, held off the attackers until they withdrew, perhaps because they anticipated the arrival of the security forces. These, when they came, gathered the nuns and those pupils who had not taken to the bush, into the priest's house, which they surrounded with guards. There with the bullet holes of the previous fusillade showing clearly in the walls, the nuns, stunned by the attack and the deaths of their fellow missionaries, waited with their terrified pupils for the dawn. Next day the security forces insisted that the mission be abandoned, and that the place be cleared by 10.00 am, a decision which the local bishop endorsed. The nuns cooked breakfast for their pupils, for the soldiers, for the African helpers, for the pupils trickling in from the bush and for themselves. Then they began to gather together what few things they could take with them. In this they were interrupted by the arrival of a priest from the next mission. His chief concern was that the consecrated hosts in the tabernacle be consumed, a task which he thought that the resident priest, overcome by the deaths of the two brothers and the abandonment of the mission, might forget. There happened to be a great many hosts in the tabernacle, so he sent for the nuns to help him consume them. When they obediently arrived he sent them back to fetch a glass of water each. They duly went off to the water supply, which was at some distance, returned with their glasses of water and prepared to receive the hosts. What they received as they waited clutching their glasses of water, was a long sermon on the feast of the day, that of the Ugandan Martyrs. After a sleepless and terrifying night, still reeling from the shock of the deaths and the instructions to abandon their laboriously established mission, nervously conscious that the soldiers wished to get them away while they were reasonably sure that the road was not mined, the seven nuns sat and sat. 'How long', I asked the nun, one of the seven, who told me the tale, 'did the sermon last?' 'I don't really know', she said, 'It may have been only ten minutes, but in the circumstances it seemed like two hours'.

There are times when the only sermon suitable for this congregation on this occasion is no sermon at all.

5

Clarity, Simplicity and the Steeplechase at World's End

One evening in the course of a social gathering at the Oxford University Chaplaincy a woman came up to me and spoke appreciatively of a sermon she had heard me give on the Feast of the Assumption. The setting of that sermon was unusual. It was delivered in the social club at Harwell, the lair of the Atomic Energy Authority, where I had been asked to say a midday mass. I remember a long, handsome table which reached almost from wall to wall, across which I faced a couple of dozen Catholics who worked in the establishment. It was several years later that I was to hold my dialogue with the Wolf Cubs of Rhyl on the significance of that same Feast of Assumption. How interesting, or possibly embarrassing, it would be to have recordings of both occasions. When I sat through my seminary course on Mariology it never crossed my mind that I would one day have to treat of the doctrine of the Assumption with boys of nine and ten and also with people engaged in nuclear research. Yet that degree of versatility is just one of the demands made of priests and, for some, a minor one at that.

Relative Depth

At Harwell I knew that I both could and should treat of the doctrine of the Assumption at some depth. With the young wolf pack I was aware that I must speak in their words and use their mental categories, which I did, having got them to speak first. Facing a typically mixed parish congregation the relative depth at which you should deal with your theme can be very hard to gauge. I am therefore glad to report that a number of my correspondents consider that their clergy pitch the level correctly. Of the few expressing some dissatisfaction not one complained that their clergy were too intellectual or talked over the heads of their people. One judged that 'the bishop is rather complex and slightly obscure'. Two others complained of 'obscurity', but they were criticising the presentation rather than the intellectual level of the material.

Two qualities in a sermon which my commentators rate highly, indeed which they demand, are clarity and simplicity. They are right to value those qualities, but I wonder if they realise how much they are asking of us, especially when they insist that we should always be 'simple'. Not that clarity comes easily.

Clarity

All communications should be clear. A road sign should be easy to see and read and its meaning obvious; the instructions on the medicine bottle should leave us in no doubt how much to take and when. We should be clear when we give guidance in the confessional, clear when we offer advice outside of it, clear when we give doctrinal instructions. I am not saying that every statement we make must be neatly cut and dried, a matter of black and white. If a matter is complex we should make it clear that it is so. If a thing is uncertain, we must make the degree of uncertainty clear to the hearer. If something is delicately nuanced we should do our best to point out those nuances. When I tackle such mysteries as the Trinity or the Hypostatic Union, I should try to advance my hearers' understanding and to give them further insight, without leaving them with the impression that the matter is now wrapped up. Too many of us left school, and a regrettable proportion of us the seminary, thinking that because we could say 'One God, but Three Persons' and 'Two Natures, but One Person', we thereby had these issues nicely under control. It is my mission to help people to see as far as they can into the depths of what God has revealed; I must never present that revelation as a shallow pool.

Steps To Clarity

How do you produce clarity? The first step is to get the matter perfectly clear in your own mind. Much of my own education, both secular and theological has come not only from gathering material for my classes and congregations, but from the subsequent effort to get the material utterly clear in my own mind before offering it to the minds of others. If your own thinking is at all fuzzy and vague, your exposition will be even fuzzier. Then you will soon be in the ditch, taking your hearers into its muddy waters with you. The second step is to find the words and the illustrations which will make the material as clear to your congregation as it is to you. At this stage you may well find that you understand the matter rather less well than you thought, and that when you step outside the accepted technical phrases you are quite at a loss what to say. The experience is painful, but salutary. Persevere, and the effort will benefit both you and your congregation.

How are you to know what your congregation will find clear in the way of words and illustrations, and what is more likely to baffle them? This is largely a matter of experience, of experience in the first place of the type of people who make up your congregation. It comes from your talking with them, still more from listening to them, from your acquaintance with the programmes they watch on television and the periodicals they read. Secondly, you rely on your wider experience of talking to people, whether in groups or as individuals, of giving them information, of explaining to them, of sharing your attitudes with them.

It was simpler in the classroom. There I could test the efficacy of my explanations by asking questions, and pupils could, if puzzled, put their questions to me. As a preacher I dare not do the first — much as I am tempted! — and to my regret, congregations will not do the second. Yet the teacher does not rely entirely on questions, his/her own or those of the pupils. Teachers develop a sense, acute in some of them, less so in others, of whether a class understands or not. A preacher can develop a similar sensitivity. You can acquire a feel for the attention, for the comprehension or otherwise of a congregation. You can learn to observe and interpret their facial expressions, their bodily postures and their movements. Preachers, like teachers, become receptive in this way if they are really interested in their hearers, if they are willing to invest attention and energy in observing them. The price can come quite high. To focus on what you are saying, to monitor without respite the way you are saying it, your voice and gestures, and at the same time to observe the congregation − all of the congregation − closely, adds up to a considerable expenditure of energy. It has been well spent if it helps to make the word of God a little clearer to the People of God.

Clarity and The Clever

One evening in the days when I was a Deputy-Headmaster there came to my room a discouraged first year teacher. He had that day introduced his class of thirteen-year olds to the Latin construction known as the Ablative Absolute. He had spent most of the period explaining and illustrating. Then he tested the class with a few questions and found to his dismay that none of them had been able to follow him. 'What do I do?', he asked. 'I've never had any difficulty understanding anything'. I believed him without hesitation. He had left school with an Oxbridge award and at the University had gained a Double First. It was interesting to hear what could be read as an arrogant assertion spoken as an admission of helplessness. Quite different was the experience of a contemporary of mine pressed during an emergency and almost without warning into teaching Mathematics to the younger boys. He found the assignment formidable and often had to consult his colleagues, but the Senior Maths Master was quite satisfied. 'X makes a good teacher for those boys', he said, 'because he has the same difficulties as they do'.

Does it follow from my two stories that a considerable intellectual ability and a high academic standard are a liability in a teacher, and, for that matter, in a preacher? 'Me genoito. Let it never be so!', as St Paul says whenever his argument seems to be taking him in a direction in which he does not wish to go. The person with considerable knowledge and highly developed intellectual powers has a rich store of facts and insights to share. The snag appears, as my Oxbridge scholar found out in the actual process of sharing. The mind of the scholar moves easily and usually swiftly among abstractions, technical terms and fine spun logic. Most of us think more slowly and do so in the concrete; we are unversed in technicalities and quite unused to drawn out argumentation. The scholar or the intellectual has therefore to build a bridge from one plane to the other, to transform the abstract into the concrete, from technical terms into common language, to abridge and simplify, and all at a slower pace.

Some intellectuals do seem incapable of moving out of their own bookish, theoretical mental confines. I knew a well educated, very articulate parent whose small son had a phase of near-anorexia. The parent anxiously delivered him a series of lectures on dietetics. The chemistry was accurate and the arguments unanswerable. The child's food remained on the plate. Other academically successful people use their developed intelligence to grasp the problem and find solutions. They apply their imagination and their capacity to handle complex information, so as to enter into the outlook and situations of people whose circumstances differ very much from their own. They call on their mental dexterity and verbal skill to modify their vocabulary, produce apt illustrations and select the right depth, pace and length for their exposition. At the comprehensive school in which I once had the privilege of attempting to teach, the Head of Mathematics and the Head of English were people of conspicuous intelligence and broad culture. They both moved between the Sixth Form and the least academic juniors with practised ease and equal effectiveness.

Never fall for the Philistine propaganda which maintains that academic and cultural pursuits disqualify you for dealing with 'the simple faithful'. Never believe that if you keep your serious reading to the minimum and talk football, cars and clerical gossip you will be the more able to handle 'the real world of ordinary people'. There was quite a pocket of that school of unthought among the seminarists a little senior to myself. I used to listen attentively to the practice sermons of my fellow students to hear what material and style they considered right for the 'ordinary' congregation. I found the less academic for the most part the less able to get away from technical terms and religious clichés. They lacked the mental dexterity to get behind the habitual formulae and sometimes, I suspected, the wit to see the need for doing so. The most direct, cliché-less, untechnical lucid piece came from the student with the highest I.Q. in the place. At present he is the Rector of the Jesuit house for post-graduate studies in Rome.

Simplicity

One of my correspondents says at the end of her comments, 'However difficult the subject or deep the thought, the explanation must be simple and so intelligible to all'. I take this comment especially seriously because the writer is a greatly respected doctor in general practice. No matter how complex a disease or involved the treatment, she has to find a simple description and a set of instructions 'intelligible to all' to offer to the patient. She has the right therefore to expect a parallel skill in a preacher.

I do not find simplicity a simple matter to discuss. Would the reader find it a simple matter to define simplicity? The nearest dictionary to hand says, 'Not compound, consisting of one element, all of one kind ...'. A few paragraphs back I said, 'It was simpler in the classroom', meaning that it was a straightforward, uncomplicated process to find out whether a class was following me. So, a process, a notion, an explanation are simple when there is not much to them. Can one be 'simple' if the matter to be explained is complex or somewhat nebulous? Sometimes you can break the thing down into units which are easily grasped one by one, making sure that each point is clear and so being careful not to move from point to point too fast that the interconnection of the unit is understood. Even this carefully organised process makes quite a demand on the listener's concentration.

One learned colleague, when I broached with him my problems with 'simplicity', delivered himself of the magisterial dictum, 'All great art is simple'. He obviously considered that he had settled the matter. I went away wondering whether I had heard a very wise observation or a glib slogan. Are 'King Lear', Eliot's 'Four Quartets' and the music of Beethoven simple? The adjective does not immediately spring to mind, especially with regard to the 'Four Quartets'. An effective work of art always has unity. The mind of the writer, artist or composer has imposed a powerful coherence of part with part, a dynamic collaboration between the various components which give it an almost organic oneness. Does that unity confer simplicity? It certainly contributes to it.

Can something of this sort, i.e. a relative simplicity based on an all-pervasive unity, be achieved in a sermon? I like to think so. When my schoolboy debaters were preparing their speeches I insisted that they be able to state the 'thrust' of their argument in one sentence with a single main verb. Thus in a debate in the sixties on the Common Market the 'theme sentence' of one boy ran, 'To join the Common Market is to sacrifice our more productive, more international, more promising ties with the Commonwealth'. That of another boy: 'The Common Market is a cumbersome bureaucracy very like an armoured car with insufficient horse-power and over-powerful brakes'. I urged the lads to keep these sentences clearly in mind throughout the composition of their speeches and during the actual delivery. If they did, the speeches had unity, the subordinate points, the examples, the details being plainly seen to build into a single case. To apprentice speakers I have often given the same advice, 'Be ready to sum up the point of your sermon in one sentence with a single main verb'. Where this advice is followed the resulting sermon has unity and is easier to follow and absorb. Is it thereby simpler? If you define 'simple' as 'not compound' as 'not having parts' then a sermon with a fair amount to it can hardly be simple. Yet, if the parts plainly fall into place and the overall unity is apparent, the sermon becomes in some sense simple.

Looking back over the last two paragraphs I see such phrases as 'powerful coherence', 'dynamic collaboration' and 'an all-pervasive unity'. Agreeably mouth-filling and satisfyingly resonant phrases they certainly are, and I would claim, logically deployed. Do they convince? With me abstractions, no matter how plangently they resound, no matter how cogent the logic with which they are marshalled, never quite strike home. So, I have issued myself with a dare, or, in more exalted language, quixotically imposed on myself a formidable challenge. I have asked myself how I would tackle a sermon on Luke 21, 5–36. This is a real dragon of a passage, obscure, involved, highly coloured, not to say lurid, its apocalyptic, eschatological rumblings breathing menace. Could I expound that passage without distortion, without significant omission, with scrupulous honesty and yet achieve simplicity, or come anywhere near to doing so?

Two concessions I have made to myself. First the passage being overlong for a single sermon, I have allowed myself more material than I would normally attempt to cover in a single address. Secondly, I am not going to set out a detailed plan of a sermon with introduction, examples, applications and conclusions, but simply (simply?) indicate the lines along which I would try to deal with this formidable topic. I shall put into parentheses my comments on two particularly problematic verses, because in a sermon I would separate them by my words, my manner, my tone from the rest of the address, so that they would not confuse the general development of the whole.

In the first place I WOULD TRY TO MAKE THE PASSAGE LOOK LESS DAUNTING by raising the possibility that the speech is actually *a collection of remarks* made by Our Lord on different occasions, which the gospel writer has brought together in this one context. The congregation is not obliged therefore to imagine Jesus thundering on at length about death and destruction, 'distress of nations' and 'men fainting with fear and forboding'. I would add that the early Church could stomach large helpings of this sort of language because they knew how to take all the *apocalyptic stage props*, the earthquakes, the terrors, the signs in the sun and moon. They were familiar with this style of literary presentation which was widely used by both Jewish and pagan writers to bring out the serious nature of an occasion or series of events.

Here I would use the story of Pentecost. Peter, explaining the situation to the crowd who had heard the disciples speaking in tongues, said '. . . this is what was spoken by the prophet Joel:.

I will pour out my Spirit and they shall prophesy.
And I will show wonders in the heaven above and signs on
  the earth beneath,
blood and fire, and vapour of smoke:
the sun shall be turned into darkness and the moon into blood'.

The ecstatic disciples were there to be seen and heard, but nobody was seeing, or had seen, any of Joel's intimidating cosmic phenomena. Nor did they expect to. It was not that they took such language less than seriously; they took it *seriously, but not literally*. It signified for them God's special action in the realm of His relations with humanity, not in the physical world. We today do not have 'apocalyptic' language, but we do have metaphorical language and poetic expressions. We say: 'He has nerves of steel', 'the exhibition was out of this world' and 'she is broken-hearted'. These statements are not literally true, but we are still saying something quite meaningful about his courage, the quality of the exhibition and her distress.

WHAT underneath this sensational, melodramatic language IS OUR LORD SAYING?

Some of his companions were admiring the Temple with its splendid buildings still being added to, and its rich decoration of gold, bronze and tapestry still accumulating. Jesus warns them soberly that *this fine edifice will meet with total destruction*. They quite naturally want to know when, and he replies, this time with a generous measure of apocalyptic, that there will be *other important events first*.

There will be *false prophets* of the end of the world, whom they must avoid, and fierce *persecution* which they will have to endure.

I should feel obliged to mention the contradiction between v.16 'some of you they will put to death' and v.18 'not a hair of your head will perish'. Perhaps the second verse has strayed from its original place. Perhaps it is a metaphorical way of saying that the persecution will leave them untouched spiritually.

Sometime after the persecution will come the bloody *siege and destruction of Jerusalem* and the Temple with it.

Separate from these events is the *Second Coming of Christ*, which we would term the End-Of-The-World. For most of us the end-of-the-world is an uncomfortable thought. We think of ourselves being judged, of being found publically guilty of our various lapses from Christian standards with just the two possibilities of Hell and Purgatory before us. The Jews and the early Christians saw the 'Day of the Lord', the coming of the Kingdom of God in its fullness, very differently. For them it was everything you could hope for. Evil would be shown up for what it is, and the good would come into their own everywhere and forever. God's happy ending was to affect every level of life and be on a cosmic scale. It could not come fast enough.

At some time I would have to face the disconcerting verse (32) 'this generation will not pass away till all has taken place'. This sounds as though the Second Coming was to take place in the lifetime of Jesus' hearers, which it obviously didn't. I would point out that when Luke's gospel took final form, Jesus' generation had already passed. Yet Luke writing down this, to us very confusing statement, leaves it without comment. He and his generation, presumably had an understanding of 'this generation' or of the implications of 'all' which is now lost to us.

WHAT behind its lurid technicolour *DOES THIS* steeplechase of a DISCOURSE *SAY TO US* who live long after the Roman destruction of Jerusalem, for whom the Second Coming is perhaps round the corner, but perhaps still millenia away? I suggest it is saying this: *our lives are very important*; they are part of the great drama of God and humanity; our choices are significant; we can move to destruction with Jerusalem and its Temple, or we can be a triumphant part of the great Happy Ending, which itself will have no end.

We must *expect hostility* from a non-Christian world, and possible betrayal by those closest to us (which I would stretch to fellow Christians acting from un-Christian motives), and the ever downward drag of our own self-indulgence and worldliness. We should live vividly aware of the importance of our Christian lives (expressed in the hyperdramatic symbolism of the discourse), always aware of the forces opposing us from without ('you will be hated by all for my name's sake') and within ('take heed to yourselves lest your hearts . . .'), *resolutely holding on* under persecution ('By your endurance you will gain your lives') and temptation ('praying that you may have strength'), and *confident in Christ* who will undoubtedly come 'with power and great glory', whose words 'will not pass away'.

I set myself a final test. Can I do what I so nonchalantly tell my apprentice preachers to do, and express the 'thrust' of my sermon in a single sentence with only one main verb. Here is my attempt.

This passage is telling us through its dramatic symbolism that our lives, poised between total destruction and eternal fulfilment:

> *require us to be vigilant,*
> *courageous in the face of hostility,*
> *tenacious in time of temptation,*
> *and confident in the power and fidelity of Christ.*

I have already referred to this gospel passage as a steeple-chase. I did so remembering my boyhood visits to Aintree on Jump Sunday, i.e. the Sunday before the Grand National. On that day the citizens of Liverpool would tour the course gazing in awe at the height and breadth of the fences and the almost vicious ingenuity of Becher's and Valentine's. In the eschatological discourse the Synoptic evangelists have presented preachers with a similarly hostile course. It is not enough for the preachers to clear the fences themselves; we have to take the congregation over them as well. The reader must judge whether I have taken my fences cleanly, whether I have gone round some of them and whether the congregation would have been thrown from the saddle.

I took this passage to test whether, if I worked hard to give my exposition coherence and unity, I might achieve something in the nature of simplicity. My correspondent said, 'However difficult the subject or deep the thought, the explanation must be simple and intelligible to all'. Do you think, would she have been satisfied, with my handling of this eschatological discourse? Are you?

6

Preparation De Luxe

For five of my years as a teacher chaplain I lived in the same house as a retired lecturer in catechetics, an unsung hero of the pioneering period of that subject. By this time he was nearing seventy, but still with the vigour to grow fruit and vegetables on his Council allotment. He used to say masses in school, help with confessions and was always willing to deliver an incisive, up-to-date talk to parents or local teachers on the subject of religious education. The one thing he would never do was take a class. We had thought that he might wish to dabble occasionally, to experiment a little in the actual practice of his subject. He declined absolutely. He wanted no classroom contact whatsoever. It says much for the respect in which he was rightly held that this resolute avoidance of the practical did not undermine for us his credibility as an expert in the theory. But how different it would have been, how warming, how encouraging for us, if he had been at least sometimes, seen to hanker after the classroom. If he had discussed with us a little nostalgically our daily struggles at the chalk face, or wistfully recalled his own!

The reader cannot complain of any such reluctance to reminisce in myself. I am forever trotting out for inspection my experience in classroom and pulpit and my amateur attempts to coach speakers and preachers. I do this for two reasons. First, for me it is the concrete example which convinces while abstractions rarely do so. Secondly, all that I have to say about preaching springs directly from my experience and has no other source whatsoever. I am always ready therefore to take the reader, into my

66

workshop and display the materials and the methods I employ. One particularly important piece of apparatus, perhaps the most important of the lot, is my method of preparation. I shall exhibit the de luxe model, the one I employ when there is plenty of time in which to prepare. Of course, that situation is about as frequent as a total eclipse, but it is this de luxe model which shows most clearly the method I always follow. It presents my ideal and brings out the principles behind the practice. My procedure in more workaday circumstances is to my regret, only a cut down version, sometimes a mere stump of that ideal.

The Subconscious Simmer

I believe in initiating the process of preparation as soon as possible, no matter how distant the delivery date. At Oxford an invitation to preach at the principal Sunday Mass in the Catholic Chaplaincy always came a term in advance. This very efficient arrangement meant that the interval between receiving the invitation and actually preaching was a matter of some months. Each year during my six years in Oxford I received such an invitation, and on each occasion I looked up the readings for the relevant Sunday the day after the invitation came. Many weeks would pass before I deliberately turned my mind to those texts again. This process I always thought of as 'putting it on the back burner'. When months later I took the material off the back burner and put it under the full heat — such as it is — of my mental grill, I always found that the cooking process was already underway, thanks to that long subconscious simmer. Some section of my mind had been worrying at those texts, examining them, coming up with questions and suggestions.

When I was a full time schoolmaster I had to work to a more contracted timescale. Then, if I were to preach on Sunday, I would read through the texts on Tuesday, but only start to study them on Friday night. At one period of my life, when I had an under-organised Superior, I would look up the coming Sunday readings every Tuesday, lest I be suddenly asked at supper on Saturday night to take a public mass the next morning.

Reconnaissance

At Oxford I knew the Chaplaincy congregation well enough, because we lived in the next street and I often went to Mass at the Chaplaincy. In different circumstances I would be in a hurry to learn about the congregation. If the invitation was oral I would immediately interrogate the inviting priest. Given time and opportunity I would supplement this information by consulting someone else who had preached in that church. Best of all I liked to come across a worshipper at that particular church. Should the three descriptions not coincide, I was inclined to put my money on the third. Nor did I forget the second half of the master formula 'this congregation on this occasion'. Was I being asked to preach at a Unity Service, on some anniversary or on a perfectly ordinary Sunday? To repeat the military dictum already cited, 'Time spent on reconnaissance is seldom wasted'.

Study

Having gathered all the information I could about the congregation and occasion, I would deliberately put both out of my mind for the next stage, which is that of study. This is when I get down to the subject matter, reading, thinking, brooding, questioning colleagues, discussing with friends, tapping any source of knowledge or understanding to hand. I have termed this activity 'study', which could suggest a pleasant browse among the books. It is nothing of the sort. I usually find it a hectic struggle against the calendar. I feel like Jacob at the ford, struggling all night against a superior opponent, battling to win a blessing from him. The blessing in my case is to enter into the scriptural text, to appreciate its depth and implications and to respond appropriately. It is not enough to understand the text as though I were doing an exercise in superficial translation. I am engaged with literature, and with religious literature at that. To literature one must respond with one's imagination and one's emotion; to literature which is the revealed word of God I should be much more sensitively alert and more deeply receptive.

Throughout this period of study, and only during this

period, I put aside all thought of the congregation. I must first understand for myself, perceive and appreciate for myself, so that these experiences are genuinely my own before I attempt to share them with others. How long do I spend on this phase of my preparation? That depends on the amount of time there is. I never feel that this part of the process is complete; I move on nevertheless, because there is so little time left, and most of the process still to be tackled. So I come to CHOICE.

Choice

From this point onwards I try to keep the congregation continually in focus. Every decision must be made with them in my sights. The first of those decisions concerns the matter of my discourse. What is there in my understanding, appreciation and application of the readings which is likely to be of service to this congregation on this occasion? Then, how much of what I think would be serviceable is it feasible for me to include in a single sermon? What is the best point or points for me to develop? If I decide on a single point, what are to be the main lines along which I should develop it? If I aim to make several points, in what order shall I put them? By this process of selection I hope to arrive at the SKELETON. Then the skeleton must be given FLESH, i.e. I must find phrases for the pivotal concepts, choose examples, decide on an introduction, consider a conclusion and decide how to move smoothly from one section to the other. During this period of CHOICE I should be moving towards the formulation of my THEME SENTENCE. I explained in my last chapter that I ought to be able eventually to put the thrust, the gist of what I have chosen to say into a sentence with a single main verb. If I cannot form such a sentence then my thinking is not yet ready for transmission to others.

Crystallisation

At this next stage I am trying to pull everything together, to make the final decisions about matter, phrases, examples, etc. At one period in my life I never seemed able to reach this period of crystallisation until five minutes after midnight with the sermon to be given in the morning. The ideas, phrases, illustrations would be swirling round in my head like the washing in a tumble dryer, until, as desperation began to set in with the passing of midnight, the whole mix would begin to take shape. I would pace nervously up and down — not if there was anybody living underneath me — mentally tidying up, and then tumble into bed feeling that I had a sermon if only I could get it fixed in my head before mass. If I make NOTES before preaching, I do so only after this stage of consolidation. Breakfast and the period after breakfast were often spent scribbling. I felt, and must have looked, like a dilatory schoolboy now desperate to get his homework written up before class.

Memorisation

After the process of crystallisation comes the work of MEMORISATION. I have to make certain first of all of the sequence of ideas. Next comes 'linkage', i.e. the smooth transition from point to point. Lastly I try to commit to memory the key phrases and examples, which if I have the outline quite clear, does not present much difficulty.

The Conscious Simmer

For me the work of preparation is never complete. I go on thinking about the approaching sermon, mulling over the points, recalling the linkage, the phrases and applications, mentally rehearsing and re-rehearsing. Even at this stage my mind may come up with a more telling adjective, a more incisive expression. As at the very beginning of the whole operation I put the text on the back burner to simmer, so towards the end of the process I keep what I have prepared simmering on a low light, this time on a front burner. I have two reasons for doing this. First, I am terrified of forgetting. I put on my vestments in the sacristy horribly certain that I am still a long way from having a real grip on my material, and morbidly sure that I shall lose my way, stumble and omit whole sections of my discourse. This, mind you, is my fourth decade as a priest! Secondly, just as food is at its best when it comes straight from the oven onto your plate, so my preaching loses something when I have switched my mind to something else, and come to the pulpit or lectern with my material 'going cold'. At one period of my life I used to preach two or three times a term in the Leeds University Chaplaincy, speaking at both the morning and evening masses. After tea on Sunday evening I always spent at least an hour revising the morning's sermon so that it arrived 'fresh' in front of the evening congregation. The second delivery was usually rather better than the first. I used to think that the ideal form of final preparation would be to deliver one's sermon to a small, friendly congregation on Saturday night, discuss it with them afterwards, adjust accordingly and serve an improved, tested version on Sunday.

That would be a super-de-luxe formula for preparation. The circumstances I have described are already luxurious enough in terms of energy and time. I hope that the reader is not under the impression that all my preaching has been prepared in situations of abundant leisure. Once I attended the requiem of a former tutor to whom I was much indebted. I was standing in the sacristy vested for concelebration when the parish priest came up to me and articulated the fearful formula, 'You will say a few words, won't you Father?' Outside in the church waited a sizeable congregation of the deceased's family, friends and colleagues, including a large section of his University colleagues. One person I had glimpsed as I came in was a Regius Professor, a canon of Christ Church. Was I to go out there and celebrate my friend in a thin, stumbling, generally awful attempt at a homily before a congregation habituated to the highest standards of both matter and presentation? How badly it would reflect on the Roman Catholic Church, the Society of Jesus and the Hall of which I was Master! I looked at the clock. There were nine minutes to go before the ceremony began. I gave the only possible answer. 'Right-ho', I said.

Thank goodness that sort of thing has not happened often. Nor, on the other hand is it at all common for me to have at my disposal the time which my de luxe model would seem to require. Most of my preaching over the years has had to be prepared in a very brisk and skimping fashion. I have exhibited the de luxe model, dismantling it before you to show at their clearest the principles on which I approach the job. Even a brief preparation should, I believe, contain most of the stages I have described. Let me set them out:

Reconnaissance   of congregation, occasion and place

Subconscious Simmer   of reading(s) or subject

Study

Choice   of (a) Skeleton i.e. main points
                                       (b) Flesh i.e. phrases,
                                             examples, introduction,
                                             conclusion, linkage
                                       (c) Theme Sentence

Crystallisation

Memorisation   of order of points, linkage, key
                                   concepts, phrases and examples

Conscious Simmer

You will not be surprised to learn that the lived experience of preparation is often a good deal less orderly and distinctly less logical than in my scheme. The stages spill over into one another both backwards and forwards. Information about the congregation may come to one at any time, and is not to be disregarded on the grounds that the Reconnaissance phase is complete. I may look at a congregation and decide that it is larger, smaller, younger or older than I had been given to expect. Such a last minute assessment may call for some quick adjustment. The process of Fleshing will not always wait until the Skeleton is fully articulated. If I am lucky, apt phrases and examples may start suggesting themselves well before I have settled on the order of my points. On the other hand, a better phrase, a better comparison, a neater transition between paragraphs may present themselves during the Conscious Simmer. They may even come as one is speaking. The activity of Choice is never complete until you have spoken the last syllable. This is particularly true of the last paragraph. Listening to myself and watching the congregation, I may decide on adjustments, softening something which sounded a little harsh, if possible, putting more clearly those points which sounded a little vague, or repeating a little more emphatically something which I feel has not really gone home. In the end a sermon has to be made to fit this congregation, not as I thought it would be, but as I find it this minute.

Notes, If You Must

You may have spotted that under the heading Crystallisation I wrote only of Notes, ignoring even the possibility of writing the sermon out in full, and treating even the making of notes as optional. My belief that a sermon should remain 'plastic' as it were, until the last word has been spoken, is only one of my reasons for discouraging the apprentice speaker, usually without success, from composing a complete script. A more important reason is that if you write out the sermon in full you are liable to think that your piece of paper is the sermon. This attitude betrays itself in the phrases like 'I am halfway through my sermon' meaning it is half written, and 'I have finished tomorrow's homily' when you have composed your last sentence. A written paper, no matter how eloquently worded, no matter how neatly drawn up in paragraphs, is no more a sermon than the printed text of a Shakespeare play equals the drama staged. A drama takes place, and so does a sermon. A sermon is an event involving you with the congregation and them with you, God's grace, one hopes, being at work in the minds and hearts of both. 'I have finished tomorrow's homily', puts the focus on your engagement with a piece of paper, instead of on your engagement with the congregation.

But No Essays, Please

For the inexperienced preacher there is another danger in writing out the sermon in full. You will probably compose not a sermon, but an essay. For most of us essay writing was dominant throughout our education at both secondary and tertiary levels. As a result, put us in front of a piece of paper with a pen or typewriter and a topic and we will try to write an essay. The differences between an essay and a sermon are considerable. An essay is something you write for another person to read. The reader goes through it at his or her own rate, slowly perhaps at the more difficult bits, going back and re-reading what was not grasped first time. A sermon is something people are going to listen to — you hope! You choose the speed of delivery, which is therefore the same for all of them. They have to catch your meaning first time. (I should love some member of the congregation to say, 'Please, Father, can you say that bit again?'). The style of a sermon has to be different from that of an essay in the construction of its sentences and even to some extent in vocabulary. If you must write the whole of your sermon out in full, say each sentence out aloud and listen to it. Try to put yourself in the position of someone who does not know what is coming. The fact that you can with an effort get your mouth round the words is not enough. Your congregation is not normally going to sit on the edge of their seats straining to follow your verbal contortions. I once coached a lay preacher whose typescript of her homily contained a number of long, straggling, broken-backed sentences. She thought that because she could actually plod her way through them, they must be adequate. I fetched a tape-recorder and played them back to her with comment. It was a difficult job to do tactfully, and I don't think that I quite succeeded, but her sentences definitely improved.

Another disadvantage of writing out your sermon in full is the danger that you will read it out in the presence of your congregation and not speak directly to them. You may find yourself declaiming your words into the air, or worse still, delivering them into that piece of paper on the lectern, and not addressing the congregation at all. I have to admit that the Anglican divines I listened to in Oxford always used a script. They were adept at reading it with swift downward glances and addressing every word to the congregation. I watched them with admiration, but still thought that something had been lost by the use of the script, a certain naturalness, a degree of immediacy. Also a full script tends to freeze your address, militating against that plasticity, that flexible response to the feel of a congregation and to the occasion which I spoke of above.

Imagine that you have a friend who is hesitating out of sheer diffidence to apply for a post for which she is well qualified, and which you know she would enjoy. Imagine another who is on the point of resigning such a post in a fit of pique over some minor misunderstanding with one of his colleagues. If you felt obliged as a friend to encourage the first to apply, or to dissuade the other from precipitate action, would you first of all write out your arguments word for word? Would you go along, sit down with your friend, produce your typescript and start to read to her or him. You would do well to have got your arguments clear in your own mind beforehand, to have thought of some telling parallels and perhaps to have some diplomatic phrases ready to use in the more ticklish parts. But a script or even a page of notes? Unthinkable? It is my conviction that we should aim in our preaching at that degree of directness which we take for granted when we are dealing with a friend face to face. Not possible with a large audience? Trade union speakers often achieve it. Comedians, the good ones, do it even better.

And Prayer?

When I distributed my enquiry about preaching, I also submitted to one theologically informed and catechetically experienced laywoman an outline of the method of sermon preparation which I have been describing in these pages. Her comments were hearteningly laudatory, but she put her finger tactfully on one embarrassing omission — 'I would tend to mention prayer'. That is an observation which no-one is going to oppose, certainly not I, and yet I have still made no mention of the word 'prayer', and it is plainly not present in my scheme. Why?

Let me begin my explanation with a question: where in my scheme would you insert prayer? At the very beginning? As a part of study? Before choice? For me the answer is, 'Nowhere and everywhere'. Nowhere do I make prayer a separate item, and it is my ideal, too seldom realised, to make the whole preparation prayerful. If I am, for instance, to preach on the Feeding Of The Five Thousand I do not make a formal meditation on the subject. Were I to try, I should remain aware that I have come to this subject because I am due to preach on it. I should be in quest of material. I should be interviewing the Lord for the sake of my sermon, rather than worshipping. This, I quickly add, is a private, personal attitude. I want the reader to understand it. I do not urge, or even suggest, that he or she share it. Should anyone's mind work differently from mine, by all means let them meditate formally on the passage on which they are due to preach. Let them also insert PRAYER into my sevenfold process wherever it belongs for them.

The preparation of a sermon ought to differ from the preparation of a lesson or lecture. In a sermon I am dealing with the word of God; I am to open it to the People of God and shall be doing so during the worship of God. I am handling the sacred at every point. Hitherto I have harped on the principle that I should make every decision about my sermon with the congregation in mind. Should I be less mindful of the Sender than of those to whom I am sent? Throughout the preparation of a sermon I am in the presence of God, whether I advert to it or not; the congregation is as yet only imagined. Ideally, therefore my sense of the Lord should be as sustained as the thought of the congregation. Even more so, because I deliberately exclude the congregation from my mind during STUDY. Prayer therefore belongs everywhere in my preparation. Besides this sense, as continuous as I can make it, of God, there will be explicit prayer for guidance, for inspiration, for purity of motive. That sort of prayer can be relevant at any point in the process. Perhaps, then, I should amend my dictum and say that prayer belongs in my scheme of preparation nowhere, everywhere and anywhere.

7

The Skeleton In The Sermon

'Skeleton' and 'Flesh': I must admit that these two labels, which I have placed on important sections of my preparation process, do sound a little grisly. 'Skeleton' sounds the worse, because we associate skeletons with graves, and with those who are not only dead, but a long time dead. Perhaps I should have chosen a term with less emotional resonance such as framework or structure. Yet a sermon, unlike a building or a machine, is a living organism, one to which I am both father and mother, one which I must both beget and carry to its term, and one to which a strong, well functioning bone structure is essential.

Because a sound skeletal structure − does that sound less macabre? − is important, you may well be dissatisfied with the four or five short sentences which the topic received in the last chapter. There I said, 'If I decide on a single point, what are to be the main lines along which I should develop it? If I aim to make several points, in what order should I put them?' I raised the questions without offering a single clue as to how I arrive at my answers. In fact there is no one way, no universal formula which I always follow. There is nevertheless a pattern of development which I commonly use, and by which I am always influenced. I have absorbed it from the Ignatian method of meditation.

However, there is one part of the structure, which undoubtedly comes first and which has nothing whatever to do with Ignatian prayer: the Introduction.

Beginning

One of my correspondents wrote, 'The first minute or so of a sermon is crucial for winning the attention of a congregation. I knew of one preacher in the diocese who got into the habit of bringing a visual aid into the pulpit for each sermon; e.g. one day a broom, another day a jug'. Another correspondent comments, 'The ideal sermon should always begin with a story. I come to mass with a lot of things on my mind, and I need a vehicle to help me put these things aside so I can listen. A story will accomplish that'. I would be somewhat less dogmatic than the second correspondent about the need for a story, and I should be firmly against the slavish imitation of the priest who always lugged some incongruous object into the pulpit. To copy another person's gimmick rarely works. It is the man's inventiveness and willingness to take trouble which should serve as a model. Sheer plagiarism is thoroughly unimaginative, and lazy into the bargain. Nevertheless, both correspondents rightly insist that the beginning is important and requires some special effort.

At the seminary we always had reading at table in the old monastic tradition. Occasionally, instead of the current book, we listened to a theological essay written by a fellow student. I have clear memory of a member of my own year beginning his dissertation on 'The Immaculate Conception' with the words, 'The Doctrine of The Immaculate Conception ...' At that time I had very little experience as a writer or conferencier, but I already knew beyond all doubt that this was no way to begin. I saw clearly that it was a pedagogical error. People eating their dinner, or waiting for it to be served, are not sitting there with their ears pricked to catch your first words, as though they were a bunch of journalists called to a press conference during a political crisis. The audience want to take their time tuning in to your voice, your pace, your style. They want to move smoothly into your subject, not be required to focus instantly on your first point. My colleague was not introducing his subject, he was simply starting.

Playing Yourself In

An introduction eases the audience into the context of the talk. The first couple of sentences may be quite irrelevant to the topic provided they interest the hearers and offer an easy transition to the introduction proper. Such remarks give the speaker the opportunity to monitor his or her own voice, to adjust its volume, its pitch or its tone before getting down to the meat of the discourse. They can also help you to get some initial sense of the congregation. Do they look receptive, or are they going to require a good deal of wooing? Again you have a chance to adjust your tactics. I once read that the celebrated cricketer, Donald Bradman, would sometimes walk from the pavilion to the crease, not briskly and in a straight line, but in a leisurely curve. His critics thought that he was drawing out the expectant spectators' applause. He was actually giving his eyes more time to adapt from the light of the pavilion to that of the pitch. The apprentice preacher might well learn from this Prince of Batsmen not to start hitting out before he has his eye in.

Such opening remarks can be used, not only to adjust your voice and manner, but also to work on the atmosphere a little, perhaps to take the chill off it, to remove something of the ecclesiastical starch. They can serve to disarm somewhat the wariness with which a congregation faces a strange preacher, especially one from another denomination. Once on a holiday of obligation it was arranged that I would say an evening mass in a church which I had never before seen. In the afternoon I had had some dental treatment and so arrived at the altar with one side of my face still numb from the anaesthetic. Before I began I told the congregation, enunciating my words as best I could, that I had just been in the hands of the dentist, and that with half of my face still frozen and no feeling in my tongue and lips, I could not control my speech properly. I apologised in advance for whatever distorted sounds I might emit in the course of the service. The congregation responded, listening to me sympathetically with I suspect a touch of curiosity as to how well I was going to manage. They may have been a little disappointed for in fact I coped far better than I had expected. However, my remarks did make them listen. The first time I preached in St Mary's, the University Church in Oxford, I stood a few feet away from the front bench, looked up with genuine awe at the lofty pulpit from which during the passage of the centuries a glittering array of famous ecclesiastics have preached. I said in a small, but clear voice, 'You must excuse me from going up into that pulpit. Up there I would only get vertigo at the thought of the eminent divines who have occupied it in the past ... Anyway, we trendy Papists gave them up years ago'. The laughter rang out clearly and instantaneously, and the congregation unfroze completely. It was just as well, because now I come to think of it, the text on that occasion was the eschatological discourse in Mark.

Opening remarks of this sort need to be managed very carefully. Handling the word of God is an extremely serious matter, and one must not seem to be clowning. A congregation gathered for worship, hoping for my help in their sincere efforts to follow Christ, do not want me to be flippant. I am there to serve God and to serve them by helping them to focus on the things of God, so any exhibitionism on my part can be a sacrilegious distraction. On the other hand, to poke a little fun at oneself is not to sacrifice all dignity; to get behind those Sunday faces and that churchy comportment can be a contribution to realism and not to farce. Indeed, it can sometimes be necessary to attract attention to oneself before directing it elsewhere. You are not exactly walking a tightrope, but you are venturing where there are quicksands. So tread carefully, scrutinise the ground ahead and if your foot begins to sink, get it out fast. I shall have to return to the weighty matter of the light touch later. For the moment let it suffice to say that you demonstrate your essential seriousness of purpose by the quality of what you offer, by the pains you have taken to prepare it, by the effort you are clearly making to reach and hold your hearers and by your patent involvement with the things of God. Seriousness does not equate with a po-faced demeanour.

Easing Into The Subject

In the above paragraphs I have touched upon two things: prefatory remarks which may have little or nothing to do with the subject of the sermon, and the introduction proper. The former, as I hope I have shown, can be useful, especially with a strange congregation. For a regular congregation such initial remarks may still serve a purpose, but often they can be dispensed with entirely. In contrast the Introduction proper never can. We should never ask people to focus instantly on the solid material of our discourse. You should lead them to it by stages. The commonest way is to tell a story or narrate an incident. You may try a challenging remark. You might begin with a reference to some public event or to a twist in the plot of a popular soap opera.

I often find the introduction quite hard work. To study the Sunday gospel, to reflect upon it, to get to grips with it intellectually and emotionally requires time and no little effort. In essence, however, it is a straightforward process. In contrast, to come up with an even half-attractive introduction requires inventiveness and a touch of inspiration. These are not at my command. I have to wait for them to come into play, and it can happen that they do not come at all. One reason why I like to start preparation as early as possible, is to give that elusive and unpredictable part of my mind more time in which to work. I sometimes regret the time and trouble which an introduction may cost me, but I do not regard the expense as optional.

Reviewing what I have just written I see that I have several paragraphs about the handful of sentences spoken before the main body of the sermon. That shows the importance I attach to them, and also the difficulty I often have with them. It is now high time that I began to set out the pattern of development which I normally follow in constructing the main body of the sermon. It is a pattern which I may depart from, but which always influences me. It is derived from the 'Spiritual Exercises' of St Ignatius, but it has its roots much further back in Christian meditation and preaching. Indeed, it seems to me to be rooted in the normal progression of our psychological processes.

The Three Piece Suite

During the summer months here at St Beuno's it sometimes

happens that, lying snugly in one's bed, one is jerked back into consciousness by the urgent, frenzied summons of a mechanical bell. One realises fairly quickly that the fire alarm is ringing and that either the house is on fire, or which is much more likely, some insect has penetrated a smoke detector and set it off. If the former, then I had better get up as quickly as possible for my own safety, and to secure that of others. If the latter, then I ought to get up and help to inspect the smoke detectors, to locate, clean and reset the activated one, so that the retreatants can go back to their beds reassured. Here there is a triple process:

the EVENT.............the clamour of the alarm,
the INTERPRETATION.a fire or another dratted insect,
the IMPLICATIONS....I must get up as fast as possible and help.

In the body of an Ignatian meditation (I am omitting all reference to his preludes) there is a corresponding threefold progression labelled, not very accurately:

the USE of the MEMORY,
the Application of the UNDERSTANDING,
and the Exercise of the WILL.

Ignatius' First Exercise opens with the Fall of the Angels, and it is in that context that he sets out the stages of his meditation. As a Jesuit, sensitive to my founder's reputation, I must warn the reader who has not made the 'Exercises', that the book is nothing more than an instruction manual for the director. It is therefore as eloquent and stylish as the booklet which came with the washing machine. The effectiveness of the 'Exercises' comes neither from originality of doctrine nor from the quality of the prose, but from Ignatius' acquired knowledge of the normal workings of the mind and the heart of the ordinary Christian.

His directions for the First Point in this First Exercise run:

'The First Point ... will consist in the use of the MEMORY [my capitals] to recall the first sin, which was that of the angels, and then in applying the UNDERSTANDING by reasoning upon this sin, then the WILL by seeking to remember and understand all, to be more filled with shame and confusion when I compare the one sin of the angels with the many sins I have committed'.

THE MEMORY is expected to do more than recall concrete events:

'We should apply the memory to the sin of the angels, that is recalling that they were created in the state of grace, that they did not want to make use of the freedom God gave them to reverence and obey their Creator and Lord and so, falling into pride, were changed from grace to hatred of God, and cast out of heaven into hell'.

So the MEMORY is required to recall not only the events, but the significance of those events. Their significance has been appreciated in the past and can therefore be 'retrieved'. Moreover, such terms as 'Lord', 'pride', 'hatred of God', not to mention 'cast out of heaven into hell' have a considerable emotional charge. Therefore at the stage labelled MEMORY the emotional element is already present, but it is a recollected emotion.

The UNDERSTANDING goes to work on these recollections, these 'retrieved' experiences. It revives, deepens, develops and reinforces them.

The part of the WILL is not to give emotional resonance for the first time, but to rouse 'more deeply' the emotions. The Ignatian emphasis is on the comparative 'deeper'. He also stresses at this point the application to oneself of the facts being meditated on, e.g. 'when I compare the one sin of the angels with the many sins I have committed ...'. St Ignatius does not want the effect of the meditation to end with the meditation. He wants it to influence the rest of our lives. He is hoping that the 'more deeply felt' 'shame and confusion' will make sin less attractive, even repellent, and so more resistable. We are finally in the area where we too would use the word 'will'.

The three stages of my reaction to the firebell at night form a more simple process than Ignatius' threefold movement of memory, understanding and will. I see the latter as a development of the former. The evolution has come about because Ignatian meditation deals not only with events in the past, but also with ones which I have already thought about, though perhaps superficially, and to which I have previously, though perhaps inadequately, reacted.

* The quotations are taken from the translation of Louis J Puhl, section 50.

So, the EVENT	has developed into the recall of a previous and complex experience and is termed by Ignatius MEMORY
INTERPRETATION	has developed into the revival and elaboration of my intellectual grasp of the matter, and is termed UNDERSTANDING
IMPLICATION	is now the renewal and intensification of my personal response and is labelled WILL

As I was putting together the above description of the torso of an Ignatian meditation, it came home to me anew how much it influences my preaching. It sets my objectives, even when I am far from achieving them.

Stage 1 'memory' (event)

We have seen how much work Ignatius expects from the memory. He is not for the most part proposing anything new to his retreatant. He asks him or her to mull over again what they already know, to soak themselves in attitudes which they may already have. Certainly he is hoping for a new depth, a new vigour. Of course he would welcome fresh insights and new practical applications. Yet he would be content with the recall, the retrieval of knowledge long ago absorbed, of attitudes accepted in the past, provided they are seen and felt with a new intensity.

The activation of the memory in a sermon provides us with an awkward initial problem. If I am preaching a routine Sunday homily on the gospel reading, not only has the story just been read out to the congregation, it is one which they have known for most of their lives. I must not talk to them as though they were hearing it for the first time. To serve up one's own pedestrian paraphrase of the narrative is to insult their knowledge. I will bore them and perhaps lose them right at the start. I have already quoted the group who described this particular practice as their 'pet hate', and the man who asked, 'Why put the message into a second-rate version when it is already written so much better?'

At the same time any experienced teacher knows, and any inexperienced teacher had better learn, that it is usually a mistake to take anything for granted. How then do I set the scene and recall for the congregation the actions and words of Our Lord and the other people in the story? I have to stir their memories, not do it for them. I need a tactful technique of referring to the facts rather than baldly restating them. I have to rehearse the story indirectly, obliquely bringing in the events and the dialogue rather than plodding through them. Once when I was preaching on the Presentation of the Child Jesus in the Temple, I spent a while describing the Temple, its size, grandeur, riches and thronging pilgrims. I then recalled the persons and events of the story as I contrasted the apparent insignificance of Joseph, Mary and the child in such a setting with the profound importance of who they are, what they are doing and what is said to them. On another occasion with a university congregation I set the scene of the Temptations by comparing this initial encounter of Christ and Satan, with the final scene in the classic western, where good in the form of the hero and evil in the guise of the villain, confront one another for the final showdown in the dusty, deserted street in front of the saloon. I am not commending either device to you — remember what I said about copying other people's gimmicks — but offer them as examples of how I try to recall the essential facts while avoiding an insipid regurgitation of the narrative and the dialogue.

Stage 2 'understanding' (interpretation)

Just as most of the congregation have heard the gospel story many times before, so they will have heard it commented on almost as often. Our difficulty recurs. Again, I should take nothing for granted; again I must not simply retell people what they have so often heard before, as though they had never heard the story commented on until I came along. Fortunately, the problem is somewhat less acute than with the gospel narrative. The narrative is usually more memorable than the comments of teachers and preachers on it. I still need some tactful way of restating the better known aspects. 'Besides being an example of Our Lord's readiness to forgive, this incident . . .' or 'As we are all aware, Our Lord is here proclaiming . . .' are perhaps not tactful enough, but similar, if more subtle, formulae can be found.

However, I think that the principal, if not the complete, remedy is of quite a different sort. If my comments are really my own, they will never sound quite the same as anybody else's. I do not mean that I must be original in every reflection I offer. The more I have heard and read the better, provided I have sifted through it, appreciating and responding to it personally and in an individual way. Because the material has become my own, and because it is my selection for this occasion, I will usually present it with my own stamp, in my own idiom. People will not mind if they feel that they have heard some of this before, though put rather differently.

Stage 3 'will' (implication)

The problem of familiarity diminishes when we come to the area which in an Ignatian meditation is labelled 'will'. This stage I think of as the personal response and application. The emotional response to a gospel narrative or a segment of Christ's teaching, its impact on the imagination and feelings will differ at least a little in each individual. This difference will be reflected in my reaction and consequent deductions. Nevertheless, I may still come up with trite emotional clichés and over-used, reach-me-down applications. However, there is less danger of this happening if the feelings expressed are genuinely my own and if the practical applications I suggest are the authentic product of my own reflection.

It is not originality alone that counts — although it certainly helps — but sincerity and commitment. Clichés and stereotypes will be forgiven where they are the artless expression of real conviction. Yet should they be due to my negligence or apathy, then a millstone awaits me at the margin of the incoming tide.

Concluding

Let me ask you to think for a minute about that final sentence. I am not asking whether you warmed to what is an undisguised threat, but rather whether you think that it gave the section a very definite ending.

Is there a change of rhythm and idiom from what went before?

Does it make its point firmly, clearly and even tellingly?

Is it a little less forgettable than most of the previous sentences?

I am not claiming that my sentence had all these qualities, or even a single one of them. They are the sort of factor I should look for in judging a conclusion.

I attach less importance to the conclusion than to the opening. A resounding conclusion will not win back a congregation already lost. Nor will a lame ending cancel all the benefit of an otherwise good sermon. Nevertheless, I will take some trouble, time permitting, to find a serviceable conclusion. No address, sacred or secular, should just peter out like a tap when the water has been suddenly turned off at the main. To end feebly, or just to stop like a machine when the power is switched off, seems to me disrespectful both to the hearers and to the very medium of public speech. What is more, an important pedagogic opportunity has been let slip. First impressions are important, but so is the last expression, because it is the one with which you leave people. My conclusion should establish the final tone, the standpoint at which I have been aiming throughout. Ideally, it should be my 'theme sentence' come to fruition.

One Monday in school a fellow teacher, having heard me preach the day before, remarked, 'You can tell you are a teacher. You can't preach without setting homework'. I was quite pleased. I believe that a conclusion, in spite of its name, should not have too final a ring. The subject has not been closed; it has been handed over to the congregation.

In Chapter 3, a propos of 'earthing the gospel', i.e. applying it to workaday life, I said that I no longer regard it as my duty to tell a congregation how they should put the gospel teaching into practice. 'It is my business ... to convince them that it is worth doing, but not to do it for them'. From my colleague's Monday morning remark I concluded that I had, whenever he was present, succeeded in putting the baton into the hands of the congregation, leaving them to carry it to the finish without me ... or, of course, to drop it.

Here then is the skeletal structure which I most commonly use:

OPENING REMARKS	which have no intrinsic connection with the sermon and can often be dispensed with.
INTRODUCTION PROPER	which eases the congregation into the theme.
MEMORY (Recall)	reminding people of the outline of the story or discourse. NEVER a step by step paraphrase.
UNDERSTANDING	bringing out the significance of the events, or of the verbal exchange or of Christ's teaching.
WILL (Not a helpful label)	dealing more with our response, with the implications for us, and the practical applications. (I do not think there is a neat dividing line where Understanding gives way to Will. It is more a question of a gradual shift of focus.)
CONCLUSION	a definite ending, but not a finalisation.

8

Provision For The Flesh

'Make not provision for the flesh', says St Paul in the Author-ised Version. In Chapter 6 I used the word 'flesh', not in the much discussed Pauline sense, but to signify the words, phrases, instances, etc. with which we 'flesh out' the skeleton of facts, reflections and questions which we have selected for our sermon. For 'flesh' in this sense we must certainly make provision, and in my own case it has to be very careful provision.

Being an only child, I had no siblings to talk to during my formative years. I was very nervous, unnaturally quiet and, like any only child, close to my mother. She could on some occasions speak very trenchantly, but was normally rather inarticulate with a very narrow vocabulary in which technical terms and the names of film stars underwent strange mutations. I thank her warmly now, for determined that I should be more learned than herself, she coaxed me into reading the easier parts of the newspaper when I was seven. In the same year she persuaded the local library to accept me as a member, even though at the time the official minimum age for membership was eight. As a result I built up a good reading vocabulary. Orally, however, I remained slow and clumsy. My written English was not much better, because even at the 'College', we did very little essay writing. We were too busy doing exercises in Mathematics, Latin, French and English Grammar. At the seminary it was worse. Our principal lectures were in a graceless technical Latin, as were our textbooks, while the chief examinations were conducted orally in the same barbarous jargon. Thank God I went on reading English Literature.

The turning point came in my thirty-ninth year when I was asked to write an article for a new periodical edited by two of my contemporaries. The article took me months to produce, was, to my later taste, unrelievedly ponderous and yet was followed by an invitation to write another, and then a third ... When I was forty-two my Headmaster asked me to raise a school debating team and to field public speakers. It was this combination of struggling to write articles and trying to train effective young speakers which put the whole matter of finding words, phrases and comparisons in the middle of my mental horizon. With half my life gone it came home to me that the art of the word was relevant, not only when I was writing for publication or delivering a formal speech, but every time I opened my mouth. I realised at last that were I able to put whatever was in my mind more convincingly and more arrestingly, I would reap the benefit in every context in which I operated. I should be more effective in the classroom, when dealing with boys individually, and also when interviewing their parents. I would be more persuasive at our staff meetings and even when putting my views to the Head.

Word Craft

For a priest the whole art and craft of the word in the service of the Word is even more important than for a teacher. You are forever having to give information, to explain, enlighten, encourage and exhort. You have to talk on the phone, deal with callers, visit parishioners, speak in church and in school, write for the parish newsletter, make presentations to people who are leaving or retiring and to 'say a few words' at all manner of events. Admittedly, with a little practice you can learn to 'get by' on these occasions. Yet I hope that none of my readers will ever be content to 'get by'. We should monitor ourselves in every telephone conversation, interview and address, whether delivered in church or elsewhere. 'Am I making my points clearly, tellingly, tactfully? Am I getting the appropriate tone of voice, going at the right speed? ...'. However, I am branching out too far when I should be confining myself for the present to our use of words.

The Anglo-Saxons, I believe, spoke of a 'word-hoard',

which the Oxford Dictionary renders 'treasure of speech'. We need a well stocked 'word-hoard' and should be avid to add to it. For this, one needs to read well-written books, dip into the tabloids as well as the highbrow journals and listen to accomplished speakers. Always have an appreciative ear for the pungency and picturesqueness of working class speech. (The Chaplaincy housekeeper had been complaining about students stopping up her sink with tea-leaves. As I poured her a cup of tea of my own brewing she looked at its colour and remarked, 'You can always put your four tea-leaves down the sink'. Could Tacitus have said it better?) We should watch classical drama and sometimes look at 'soaps'. We should be prepared to learn from Shakespeare, George Bernard Shaw and Groucho Marx and anyone else whose word-hoard is open for our enrichment. I would not wish you to deck out your sermons with quotations from Shakespeare, and I would certainly not want you to attempt an imitation of Groucho in the pulpit, although I should like you to relish the ingenuity and economy of his wisecracks. From Shakespeare and the other great wordmasters of our language one learns how much can be achieved with English words. Most of those same words are still at our disposal and we should handle them with care, with respect, even perhaps with a touch of awe. I cannot make literature with them, but please God let me do a decent job of conveying my meaning to others. Let me construct sentences . . .

> 'where every word is at home,
> Taking its place to support the others,
> The word neither diffident nor ostentatious,
> An easy commerce of the old and the new,
> The common word exact without vulgarity,
> The formal word precise but not pedantic,
> The complete consort dancing together.'

('Little Gidding', T S Eliot)

That ambition has sentenced me to hard labour for the rest of my life. Words come to me with difficulty, phrases are harder still, and the construction of a workmanlike paragraph can often leave me drained. So be it! Respect for the word in the service of the Word leaves me no alternative.

In the above paragraphs I have deliberately dwelt on our use of words in every context. I have done so, not as a springboard for my autobiographical reminiscences, but to emphasise my belief that effective speaking in the pulpit is only one aspect of that general verbal competence which it is our business to cultivate. Do not let yourself off by saying, 'It is the sincerity which counts, not the range of vocabulary'. Of course sincerity matters more than eloquence, and certainly more than glibness. Is it not, however, rather complacent to say, 'I can rely on my sincerity?' Does not sincerity include making use of every means available to you? An alternative excuse is, 'Some people have the gift and others haven't'. I commented in an earlier chapter on the notion of 'gift'. Here I will permit myself only two remarks. First a 'gift' will only mature with care, concentration and assiduous practice. Secondly, if you decide that you have no 'gift' for words, then you had better work that much harder to achieve without it that decent competence which both God and your people have a right to expect.

Preaching to a large congregation in a church plainly requires more formal vocabulary than one would use in a telephone conversation or an informal interview. Yet we should not become so formal as to sound unreal. I have noticed that most politicians are addicted in their speeches to using the word 'strive'. Have you ever heard anyone use the word in conversation or in a practical discussion? Trade union representatives at one time were incapable of appearing on television to defend a strike without using the phrase 'the aspirations of our members'. Words and phrases of that sort always seem to me to have a cotton wool effect, muffling the impact of whatever is being said. A preacher's vocabulary should be formal in that he or she should avoid anything in the way of slang or misplaced casualness which might jar with the dignity of the occasion. Formality does not mean using that inflated verbiage which proclaims, 'I am now standing here making a speech to you'. Words which we use only in sermons simply reinforce people's suspicion that what is said in a sermon has nothing to do with anything that happens elsewhere.

With my generation there was always a danger of using

Catholic mistranslations of technical Latin terms. Too many of us would speak of a 'grave reason', or, which sounded very odd, a 'grave inconvenience'. The Latin word 'gravis' in canonical Latin meant no more than a 'sound' reason or a 'serious inconvenience'. I once heard an Archbishop speaking on television of a 'rightly informed conscience'. That to his British audience could only mean a 'conscience working with an accurate knowledge of the facts'. The Latin from which he was mistranslating, meant a 'rightly moulded' or 'soundly educated' conscience. If you are a modern ordinand you will not have been trained with those Latin textbooks. Yet you will still make parallel blunders unless you teach yourself to do what the Archbishop obviously did not do — listen to yourself with the ears of your audience, especially if you are using technical terms. There are religious terms with which your congregation will I hope be familiar. 'Grace' and 'sacrament' are two examples. But take no chances. 'Eschatological' and 'apocalyptic' I would normally consider off limits, unless accompanied by an explanation. A well read lady of my acquaintance does know the term 'scatological', and was very surprised to hear it used, as she thought, several times in an address on the Transfiguration. Fortunately, I was also present for the talk and so could relieve her bewilderment.

In recent years some common terms seem to my ears to have acquired a special sense when used in a religious context. I hear such phrases as 'God wants us to be fully human' and 'discovering our own vulnerability', served up without comment. Is the congregation expected to know exactly what 'fully human' and 'vulnerability' mean in that context, and for practical purposes? I have wondered whether the preachers themselves had thought these terms through. Harder to spot than technical terms and vague religious clichés and therefore more difficult to eradicate, are our own pet phrases. One of my correspondents speaks of a parish priest whose weekly sermon invariably contained the phrase 'the warp and woof of our faith'. Such over-used favourite phrases do little harm provided they are not obscure or misleading. Constantly repeated however they can be an irritant.

'Stand And Deliver'

The subject of the homily chosen, the line of its development settled, and its key phrases and illustrations selected, the moment comes when one has to deliver it. It is as well if, in spite of preparation, I still feel unready. If I think that I have all my material carefully arranged and that all I have to do is to hand it over to the congregation like a postman delivering a parcel, I will be insufficiently alert and inadequately intent. A sermon does not consist of the material in my typescript or my head. It is an event which takes place between the preacher and the congregation. It has still to happen, and will require all I can put into it.

Stand Where?

Nowadays there is a question of where I deliver my homily from. From the pulpit? From the lectern? Shall I walk out from behind the lectern as soon as the gospel is read and speak from some other spot of my own choosing? Shall I sit? There is good warrant for the last. It is clear from the gospels that Christ normally gave his addresses sitting down. In the synagogue the Scripture was read standing, but the address was given seated (Luke 4.20) and the same usage presumably persisted among the Christians of early times. A bishop originally had his chair, quite literally, in the principal church and taught his people from it. That is why the principal church of the diocese is termed the 'cathedral'. The precedents are unimpeachable, but don't think of preaching from a sitting position until you are quite experienced. It is much the most difficult option. A chair tempts you to slump, and a preacher should always look alert. You must get your back and shoulders into a position which leaves your lungs completely unrestricted. Sitting also limits your gestures and you lose the freedom to move. Don't try it for some time after your ordination, and when you do, be sure that it is in a small place with an intimate setting. In a large place you can become too insignificant a figure.

You still have three options; the pulpit, the lectern or some other convenient spot. For myself, and this is a matter of taste, the pulpit is altogether too formal. I am ill at ease when abruptly elevated above the congregation,

> 'Up above the world so high,
> Like a tea tray in the sky.'

My feeling of segregation is added to by the pulpit rail. Who, I wonder, is being railed off from whom? The lectern is less of a barrier, but it is still between me and the people. So sometimes are the sanctuary steps, the communion rails, the gap between the rails and the benches, and two or three untenanted front benches. Reluctant to lob my words over this no-man's land, I often come down from the lectern, walk to the communion rails, or where the communion rails used to be and look the congregation in the eye at short range. A disadvantage of this approach is that without the lectern you have to do without notes. You can hardly hold them in front of you.

Stand How?

Wherever you elect to stand, in the pulpit, at the lectern or elsewhere, be sure to stand up straight. Do not drape yourself over the lectern; don't clutch at or lean on it. In the pulpit do not claw at its rails or surrounds. Stand free and stand up. If you are inexperienced you may feel that you are going to die during the opening sentences. Then prepare to die with your head up and your back straight. It looks a lot better, and your 'dying' words will ring out more clearly. My advice to the new preacher is, 'Stand up. Stand straight. Stand still'.

The last instruction, 'Stand still' requires a good bit of qualification. I shall have to elaborate: Plant your feet firmly so that you feel secure in at least that one respect. Then move neither foot nor hand unless that movement makes its own contribution to the effectiveness of your sermon. Never sway backwards and forwards, or from side to side. Make no pointless, repetitive gestures such as wagging the forearm up and down. Never prowl relentlessly like a caged feline. You may, and indeed ought, from a firm, still position, to make deliberate, controlled and unflinching movements which will enhance your exposition.

I once listened to two addresses by Archbishop Helder Camara. I say 'listened to', but I was not so much listening as watching. He was in movement all the time. He had an extraordinary extensive vocabulary of gestures which illustrated and emphasised his words, his moods, his appeal. That fecundity of gesture would look very exotic in a British preacher, perhaps provoking the remark I once heard made of a Mediterranean colleague, 'Tie his hands behind his back and he would be dumb'. We British think of ourselves as hardly gesturing at all. In fact we habitually use our bodies in conversation. It is not merely our facial expressions which change as we speak and respond to what others say. We nod in agreement, shake our heads in disagreement and shrug to express ignorance and resignation. We may lean forward to volunteer a suggestion or our services. People do stiffen with indignation and they also perceptibly relax their bodies with relief. That expressiveness, though far less luxuriant than Archbishop Helder's, should flow into even British public speaking. There is something quite unnatural, not to say macabre, about addressing a large audience on a subject one cares deeply about standing there looking like a statue with a tape recorder inside.

During my second year as a teacher Form 3C were the least satisfactory class. It was not a matter of discipline as they were not badly behaved. Yet, no matter how hard a teacher tried, they absorbed little of what was being taught and then managed to forget even that little in no time at all. One afternoon as I walked into their classroom the lad holding the door looked at me and grinned disarmingly, 'You should see the teachers' faces as they come into this class!' Young X seemed to gather precious little from our teaching, but he had no difficulty reading our faces before we had said a word. It is not only our faces which can be read, but our whole bodies. When I am about to preach what does my face and my stance say to the congregation? That I am glad to see them and have an opportunity to talk to them? That I am looking forward to what I am about to do? That I feel miserable and out of place? That I am about to discharge a routine chore which no longer engages me deeply one way or the other? How do you think that you ought to look? I believe that we should look quite glad to be there and reasonably eager to talk to them about something which we consider to be of importance both to them and to ourselves. People will not mind if I am initially somewhat nervous — they may even like me for it — but they will want that nervousness to give way to my absorption in what I am doing. They will want to hear the firm tone, and see the firm stance and gestures of someone who believes in what he or she is doing, who has thought something through and worked out how to express his conclusions. They do not want to relive the experience of 3C.

Nervous as we may be at the beginning of a sermon we can at least give ourselves a feeling of physical superiority by the way we stand. Security in this context begins with the feet. Place them firmly as though you were trying to grip the floor through the soles of your shoes. I prefer to put my feet about twelve inches apart with one foot a couple of inches in front of the other. This is the position I taught my boy pupils to adopt. What the graceful feminine equivalent of this posture is I leave my women readers to work out. Once my feet are in position I like to get the weight of my body forward on the ball of the foot. This gives me a feeling of being poised for action. Regrettably, I tend to overdo this movement and, as I warm to my subject, my heels tend to come right off the ground. Mind you, for Bishop Camara's second talk, I deliberately sat behind him to observe his movements. Once he had started his heels never touched the ground until the speech was concluded. I am therefore in good company.

My formula for standing up straight is to reach as high as I can with the back of my head. The back of my head, please! When I told boys to stand up straight with their heads high, they always reached up with the front of their heads, their chins sticking out like the prow of a ship. Stand up straight, but not rigid; pull your shoulders back, but not tightly. Putting the shoulders back frees the lungs; pulling them back tightly constricts your breathing. To the same end I am careful when preaching or speaking, not to wear too tight a belt, or, if in vestments, not to cinch my girdle too straitly. If you compress your stomach, the lungs do not fill as easily. The most important factor in your posture, more important than either security or dignity, is to afford those bellows on which all speech depends as much freedom and as much ease of action as you can give them.

The position of your face matters. It directs your voice and affects your vision. When I was first preaching I used to look over the heads of the back row. This ensured that I aimed my voice far enough. It was also less frightening than looking at the congregation. However, I should not recommend you to do the same. A modern congregation wants 'eye contact', which is a more normal way of talking to people. It also gives you more 'feel' for the congregation. If you are using notes you will want to look down at the lectern from time to time. You must not drop your head and read. That puts a congregation off badly, as the complaints of my correspondents bear witness. Train yourself to look down, not by bending your neck, but by swivelling your eyeballs. Does that instruction sound bizarre? I could say, 'Look down, not by moving your head, but only your eyes'. I use the term 'swivel your eyeballs' because that is what it feels like. Practise the quick downwards glance which takes in almost a line at a time. I have seen Anglican preachers go through a whole sermon reading in this way with a series of swift glances, hardly appearing to take their eyes off the congregation. To do this requires practice, as do all these techniques. It also means having your notes sufficiently high that you do not have to bend down to see them. I sometimes see a politician on television with his notes on a low table, so that he has to keep ducking down to see them. The impression given is that of a tall bird drinking. Of the two the bird looks less silly.

Let me go back to the start. You are now standing up straight, but not rigid; relaxed but alert: your feet firmly set, your shoulders back; your head up looking towards the back of the congregation. From now on make no move unless it contributes in some way to your exposition. From time to time you should turn your head to different parts of the church in order to make 'eye contact' with all the congregation. At intervals you can turn a little, changing by a few degrees the angle at which you are facing. This is best done at some new stage in the development of your discourse, so that a pause and change of position signal a new stage in your argument. All such movement should be deliberate and definite, not a restless fidgetting nor a vague shuffle. They should be easy and smooth, not a series of abrupt jerks.

Gestures need to be definite. When you make a gesture commit yourself to it wholeheartedly. A half gesture or a vague gesture gives a flavour of half-heartedness to your whole performance. A clear-cut gesture implies clarity of thought and expression. Its uncompromisingness springs from the firmness of your own conviction and commitment. Never half-do a gesture. If you are going to point, get your arm right out parallel to the floor. The important thing when making a gesture is to be aware of the position of your elbow. Lift it clear of your hip. If your elbow is lingering in the neighbourhood of your hip bone or your ribs your gesture is inadequate.

I divide gestures into two genres, the 'emphatic' and the 'illustrative'. The *'emphatic'* simply express the force of your feeling. In the days of a more robust style of preaching some preachers used to thump the pulpit at the climax of their address. Modern politicians are given to wagging their right arm up and down to emphasise their argument, a graceless, repetitive and unimpressive gesture. There are other gestures less extreme than pulpit bashing, more eloquent than the 'metronome chop'. Have you ever noticed a soccer captain signalling to his mates for more effort? I would not transfer his gestures to your church unaltered, but notice their naturalness and effectiveness.

The *'illustrative'* gesture draws a primitive picture of what you are saying. You might utter the words, 'we are so far apart' while holding out your hands as far apart as possible. If you then go on to speak of charity 'bringing us together' you can bring your hands to meet in front of you. I am not commending this particular gesture. It is for you to create gestures which will help to impress your words visually. I once preached at the evening service in a College of Education. Afterwards a lecturer came up to me and remarked, 'You can see you are a teacher. A teacher always says, "A large round ball" ...', and as she spoke she used both her hands to draw a large smooth circle in the air. I took her words as a compliment. Teachers gesture because they will use anything that comes to hand to get their point across. Should a preacher be any less eager? We have less in the way of tools, no black-board, no slides, no wall charts, no videos, no homework, no tests; (what would a test reveal about the effectiveness of our preaching?). We have to use to the full what resources we do have; gesture is one of them.

Please don't say, 'It's alright if it comes naturally, but with me gestures would be too artificial'. How 'natural' did your first attempt to walk look, I wonder. How 'natural' your first attempts to swim or to ride a bike? Is it 'natural' to be standing in a large building addressing a few hundred people? All these things require practice, perseverance, and experience. To gesture when one speaks is more natural than swimming or cycling. Give it a chance; more than one chance. And practice! A full length mirror is a great help. Perhaps your wardrobe has one, even if your sacristy hasn't. If not, one can manage with a mirror which shows the top half of one's body, although the full length image is more enlightening as to how one really appears. You may protest that to try out one's gestures in front of a mirror is repellently theatrical and narcissistic. I hope that you will listen to your voice on tape sometimes. Is the use of a mirror any different in principle? It is unlikely that you will find the tape, mirror or which is far better a video, flattering. Or is it the frankness of the tape, the mirror and the video that you shrink from? It is very understandable that you should do so. But if you do not confront your mistakes and your weaknesses, how do you propose to reduce them?

John Milton was not speaking of a woman preacher when he wrote,

> 'Grace was in all her steps, heaven in her eye,
> In every gesture dignity and love.'

Nevertheless, the lines can serve to remind all preachers that there is an eloquence of the face, of bodily posture and movement. The preacher who neglects it does so to his or her loss, and what matters far more, the loss of the gospel which it is our business to preach, and the loss of those who hear and watch us preach.

9

'Receiving You Loud And Clear'

In the last chapter I wrote, 'If you are to do your work well you need to use words well'. Substitute 'your voice' for 'words' and the statement remains equally true. On the phone, in the interview room, on your pastoral visits to people's homes, in the school, in celebrating the liturgy and other services, you will constantly be using your voice. Just as you need to monitor your wording, always asking yourself whether it is right for this person in this context, so you must always remain sensitive to your voice. Is it easily audible? Is it clear? Has it the right tone for this moment? As your choice of words in a sermon is only one facet of what I have termed 'general verbal competence', so equally your control of your voice when preaching is only one aspect of overall vocal effectiveness.

One evening a former pupil came to see me. After two years he was discontented with the job he was doing, which held out poorer prospects than the illustrated brochures had suggested. He was thinking of becoming a schoolteacher and asked for my advice. I led him from our house to the school, three minutes walk away, took him into a classroom, stood him in front of thirty-four empty desks and said, 'Imagine the full class is here. Tell them something about your present work. Speak loudly enough for the back row to hear you without having to make an effort to do so. Speak slowly enough for them to absorb what you are saying, but not too slowly'. He tried. He stood there rather miserably and delivered himself of three unenthusiastic sentences. Then he broke off, swung round to me and said querulously, 'I didn't know you had to think of all these things. I thought you just had to know your material'. 'All these things!'. I had only mentioned two. Any experienced teacher could easily have added several other factors to which you must be continually alert when in the classroom.

I had given priority to the matter of audibility because I guessed that the young man had never given it a thought. Never take audibility or clarity of speech wholly for granted, except with people who are used to you and in situations to which you are accustomed. I may well have tricks of speech peculiar to myself. These may no longer bother the people with whom I deal regularly, but they can still baffle the stranger. On the phone things are easier because the other person can always say, 'I can't hear you, Father', perhaps adding tactfully, 'This doesn't seem to be a very good line'. In the interview room people may say, 'Sorry, I didn't quite catch what you just said'. But when I am taking a service or delivering a sermon no-one is going to interrupt with, 'Will you please speak up, Father?' If only they would! One could adjust one's voice happy in the knowledge that they want to hear what one has to say. Without such interruptions how am I to know whether I am speaking loudly and clearly enough? That is another reason why I need to watch the audience. With experience it is possible to sense from people's faces and bearing whether they can hear or not. Even then my judgement may be awry, and it is well worth while to check from time to time with someone who was in the choir loft or stationed near the door.

The Writing On The Wall

My first instructor in the art of preaching was himself a dull and prosaic speaker, but a conscientious and methodical man. The combination is regrettably frequent. He had dutifully 'got the subject up', and had collected a number of quotations, some of which have stuck with me. He quoted an actor as saying, 'Use your voice to paint your words in large letters on the back wall of the theatre'. As a newly-fledged preacher I used to keep this dictum in mind, looking a little over the heads of the back row and daubing my words on that back wall with the fervour of a political dissident getting his graffito on the wall of the Town Hall before the police catch sight of him. As I gained in confidence I was able to look round my congregation and still aim my voice at the back of the church. I had already learned a similar technique in the classroom. There, even when keeping one's eye on someone in the front row, one had to be sure that one was still heard in the back row. Not only heard, but heard easily, so as to deprive the young gentlemen there of the excuse, 'I didn't hear you, Father'.

One summer term the comprehensive school of which I have such appreciative memories was rehearsing 'The Mikado'. The music, acting, movements and props were all coming along nicely, but to the producer's frustration, the actors were hardly making themselves heard two yards beyond the stage. Perhaps because he had heard me giving tongue so relentlessly at school masses, the producer asked me to help. The task proved comparatively easy. I would say to the young actor, 'In the play you are talking to him (her), but you are really speaking to the audience. He (she) already knows what you are going to say. It is the audience who need to be told. Look at him (her), but make the people at the back hear'. The youngsters caught on quickly. I had to get them to slow down their diction, and I would urge them to fill their lungs, but the work was really done once they were thinking realistically and practically in terms of the people at the back of the auditorium. The actor can face across the stage; the teacher may focus on the blackboard, though not for too long; the preacher may gaze round the congregation. All of them need to THINK UNBROKENLY IN TERMS OF THE BACK ROW, and to go on writing with their voice on the back wall as clearly, and as firmly, as a teacher drawing her diagrams in white chalk on the blackboard.

Amplifiers

I was complaining recently to one of my colleagues about the inability of a certain group of young clerics to make themselves heard at a conference. 'They would answer', said he, 'that the amplifiers weren't working properly'. This is no excuse. I have found amplifiers very unreliable. I have known them give up the ghost just before the ceremony started, or which is worse, break down in the middle. Others have insisted on giving off uncanny, menacing reverberations rather like those of a hot water system that is dangerously overheating. The ones that worked required me to keep my mouth exactly the same number of inches from the mike throughout the address; otherwise the volume soared up and dipped as one moved. Those mikes I promptly switched off. A preacher should not have to stand there motionless like some sort of reciting statue. On occasions like that, I have always been glad that I was trained to throw my voice in the old style. In one church where I used to say an occasional Sunday mass twenty years ago the technique paid off quite literally. At the end of mass an old gentleman who used to sit in the front bench, would limp slowly into the sacristy, beaming warmly, to present me with a five pound note. This was not because he had found my homily inspiring, or my way of saying mass devotional, but because he could actually hear me throughout. The resident clergy used the microphones.

I would advise you to learn to use amplifiers and not to hesitate to use them wherever reliable and unrestrictive systems are available. At the same time you must be quite capable of delivering a thoroughly audible address where no such facilities are on offer. Note that I say 'learn' to use amplifiers. I have known, and with irritation had to listen to, people who thought that amplification 'does all the work'. They were under the illusion that all they had to do was to mutter into the microphone in the usual, indistinct, half-strangled fashion in which they would talk to someone sitting next to them, and the system would convert this feeble noise into clear, agreeable, resonant sound ringing throughout the hall. What we got of course was an indistinct mutter everywhere, instead of just in the neighbourhood of the speaker. Accurate amplification registers any defects in oral technique and then exposes them to the whole auditorium. You need to speak into a microphone firmly, which is not the same as loudly, and you must enunciate clearly, but without exaggeration. In other words you need to employ a very modified version of the techniques I am about to describe.

The A B C of Audibility

Oral skills should be demonstrated and practised, rather than written down and read. Nonetheless, since my only contact with the reader is through the written word, I must make it serve as best I can. I prefer to do this, not by setting down a series of axioms, but by describing the method I evolved over a number of years of working with senior pupils, and which I have used since in modified form when assisting adults. One such adult was an ex-cook who at that time had no academic qualifications at all. He happened to mention in front of me that he had put his name down for a public speaking course which did not materialise. I promptly offered my help. No-one has ever given me better co-operation. A few weeks later he was standing at one end of a large examination hall, declaiming a Shakespearian sonnet, while I stood beyond the far door, which was as far as I could get. Clear, resonant vowels framed in carefully articulated consonants surged through the hall and enveloped me on my landing outside. The Bard would have been pleased; I was delighted.

My course evolved over the years eventually settling down into the stages listed below. I began with STANCE, a subject raised in the last chapter. I found that it gave the students confidence, made breathing easier and fostered a firm, vigorous 'attack', if I got them to:

Plant their feet firmly.

Stand straight, making themselves as tall as they could without raising their chins.

Put their shoulders back without making them taut or rigid.

To assume this position automatically before they had uttered a sound became quite quickly an invariable habit with them all.

I next tackled their BREATHING. I had them breathe in as deeply as they could, then breathe out as slowly as they were able. I showed them how you expand the lungs, not by sticking out one's chest like a pouter pigeon, but by expansion behind the lower ribs. I taught them to press with their hands on their lower ribs, and then to force their hands outward by breathing hard into the lower reaches of their lungs. I showed them how to control the outflow of their breath by getting them to sing out 'Aaaahhhh . . .', holding it for as long as possible. Through constant demonstration of these techniques my own performance improved no end, and I could breathe in and sing out 'Aaaahhhh . . .' for a whole minute, which the boys with their natural competitiveness would try to emulate. It was standard procedure at this stage for the boy to begin his practice not only by assuming the correct stance, but then taking in and slowly exhaling three huge breaths.

My next target was RESONANCE. I told the instructees to breathe deeply, to hum as powerfully as they could, and then to sing out 'Mmaaah . . .' with a violently explosive 'M'. I urged them to 'Bounce the sound off the opposite wall'. They enjoyed trying. 'To pronounce the vowel "Ah",' I told them, *'the mouth should be open* enough for one to insert two, and preferably three, fingers between the teeth'. 'Let the sound out'. I would bark. 'Pretend you're a crocodile'. I would get them to practice pronouncing all their vowels with their mouths as wide open as possible, while forming the sound correctly. It is surprising how wide you can keep your mouth open while pronouncing quite accurately a 'narrow' vowel such as the 'i' in 'it'.

The final instruction at this stage insisted on the importance of ENUNCIATION. 'You make a sound with your lungs and throat', I said. 'Then you must let it out, shaping it as it comes. You *shape it with your tongue, your teeth and your lips.* Make them all work, especially your lips'. They and I had to put quite a lot of effort into getting their lips flexible. The city lad manages to talk with extraordinarily little lip movement. With one or two lads I failed at this point, the only times I did give up on a boy. I simply could not get their upper lips moving. I dropped them from the class, not as a punishment, but because I knew that I would never be able to make speakers out of them.

I had a few sentences for practising lip work. A brief one,

I remember was 'Please be polite'. Another, which I found in a detective story, was 'Nine men's morris is filled up with mud'. There were others. My apprentice orators would take up a firm stance, breathe in deeply and out slowly three times, and then launch out on our practice sentences. I might be signalling to them from the opposite end of the room to open their mouths wider, or whispering fiercely, 'Bounce it off the far wall'. No-one over a period of more than twelve years skipped a practice. I think that they enjoyed being able to release the power in their voices, and were pleased with their growing control over how they sounded.

From the initial exercise we moved forward to reading, preferably in the school hall. The student stood on the platform while I positioned myself at the very back ('Paint your words on the back wall') and called out instructions in a voice scrupulously observant of the principles I was so sedulously inculcating. The first thing I insisted on at this stage was the right position in which to hold the text. It had to be high enough for them to read by looking down ('swivel your eyeballs') without bending their necks, and not so high as to cover any part of their faces. I also showed them that they could take in a surprising number of words with one rapid glance. For material I used poetry, commonly Hopkins, Housman and Shakespeare. Lines such as:

'Wiry and white-fiery and whirlwind swivelled snow
Spins to the widow-making, unchilding, unfathering deeps.'

demand that every consonant be rightly sounded, every vowel be given its true value. When delivered in a large room they also require very careful breath control. Further, they made good material for my next section, the awareness of and competence in managing PACE, PITCH and TONE. In private conversation most of us breathe shallowly and speak quietly, rapidly and without resonance. Thank goodness we do! Nobody wants their small living room to resound to the firm, plangent tones of public oratory. My aspirant orators had already learned to breathe deeply and to achieve a degree of resonance. Speaking in a large hall, they soon appreciated the need to speak slowly as well as loudly. They had still to learn to pitch their voices on a lower note than in conversation. 'Always', I used to say, 'start on a lower note than you were going to take'. On a lower register their voices were both more resonant and more flexible. That flexibility was certainly needed to put appropriate feeling into the poetry and to express its different moods.

I must point out here that the techniques I have described above can be modified for use in contexts other than that of the parish church. There are several types of speech between the sermon and intimate conversation. For instance, if you go into the parish school and speak to a class in their schoolroom, you must not talk to them as though you were in the pulpit. Yet it will help if you breathe a little more deeply, speak on a slightly lower note, articulate rather more clearly, and speak rather more slowly than you would when chatting to a friend. The largeish committee with a dozen or more members is another place where I have found a modified version of these techniques useful. Avoid addressing the committee as though they were a public meeting, but a deeper breath, a lower pitch, a touch more care with your enunciation, will win you a more favourable hearing in more senses than one. It is a courtesy to other members to ensure that you are distinctly audible to every one without any effort on their part. If you are at the chairperson's end of the table or room and you are addressing the chair, remember the people at the other end and make sure that they can hear you too. It is quite exasperating to be at one end of the table half hearing remarks made at the other.

Nor is what I have been urging wholly irrelevant to what has become for many the commonest form of oral communication — the telephone. Even on the phone a deeper breath will give you a firmer tone and more flexibility, while care over your consonants is rarely wasted. It is also worth bearing in mind that, because your interlocutor cannot see your face or your posture, your voice alone has to express warmth, sympathy, interest or whatever other emotion is appropriate to the conversation. I mention situations other than preaching, not because I am overly fond of ladling out advice, but because I think it important not to isolate the sermon. When we preach we are deploying in one situation the verbal and oral skills which with adjustment can serve us, and therefore be made to serve the people we serve, in a whole range of contexts.

'Intervals And Happy Pauses'

As I listened to my apprentice orators I used to play with the notion that maturity in the craft showed itself most when they were not speaking at all, i.e. in the delicately judged, accurately controlled use of the PAUSE. I was not thinking primarily of the dramatic pause, so meticulously cultivated by the florid rhetoricians of past ages, but of what I mentally label 'structural' pauses. I remember being told at an early stage of my own schooling that we should when reading aloud, stop and count one at a comma, two at a semi-colon, three at a colon and four at a full stop. There weren't any colons in our school readers, nor do I remember many semi-colons, but the formula did introduce us to the need for pauses and for having a hierarchy among them. The adult speaker requires a wider and more subtly differentiated scale of silences. If I am enunciating clearly in a large place there is, I believe, a slight, almost imperceptible, interval between words; there is quite a perceptible one after a phrase, a longer one at the end of a clause and yet a longer one – though surely not long enough to allow one to count up to four – to close the sentence. What surprisingly few people seem to realise in practice is that you need the longest pause of all at the end of a paragraph.

Paragraphing

Printers learned long ago not to present their readers with solid blocks of print running unbrokenly from the top of the page to the bottom. The page is easier on the eye with margins and with the print divided into paragraphs. A change of paragraph also signals a change of subject, or at least another aspect of the same topic. 'Oral' paragraphing, i.e. making a distinct interval at the end of a paragraph, one longer than any pause within it, is even more helpful than the printer's paragraphs. It benefits both the hearer and the speaker. It provides a brief respite for both and prepares the listener for a new development of the speaker's theme. For the speaker it is a chance to 'regroup'. If, as commonly happens, my voice has become rather shrill, I can start my next paragraph at a somewhat lower pitch. If my address seems to be dragging a little, I can change pace, brighten up my voice and manner, and perhaps make a swift decision to abbreviate my material. An intermission, even of three or four seconds, makes it much easier to 'change gears' in any of these ways. It is surprising how much rapid thinking you can do in so short a time. 'Draw a red line', I will say to a nervous first-time preacher, 'between the paragraphs'. The difference between a 'paragraphed' and an 'unparagraphed' address is as conspicuous as those red lines scored across the preacher's script.

Besides the 'structural' pause, there is the 'expressive' or emphatic pause. Today the vibrant, drawn-out, 'Ahnnddd ...' accompanied by a slowly raised forefinger and followed by a solemn would-be pregnant pause, would embarrass rather than rivet your congregation. A simple, unpretentious pause before a key word or phrase can still emphasise effectively; a moment's silence afterwards serves to let it sink in. Such devices do not belong to the basic techniques of voice control, but rather to the more sophisticated art of EXPRESSION, the use of the voice to bring out the significance and feeling which the words are meant to convey. In this area I had no progressive course of instruction and no set of axioms to offer. My trainees and I would work to put expression into the poems I brought to our practices, but soon we were engaged in the composition and rehearsal of debating speeches and public speaking pieces. They were now doing the thing 'for real'. They rehearsed; they listened to one another; they heard themselves on tape. They learned by trial and error.

Suffer Little Children

I did have one piece of general advice, 'If you get the chance, read to small children'. It is a practice I found to be of real benefit to myself. If you can do voices for the Three Bears con brio, and shamelessly invent voices for giants, wicked stepmothers and other dramatis personae, you will find the demands made on your vocal versatility by routine preaching rather tame in comparison. Perhaps the old fairy stories are no longer read to pre-literate children. Whatever is read to them in houses where people still read, I don't doubt that it will be all the more appreciated if you give it a vocally colourful interpretation. If to provide this you have to override your natural self-consciousness, so much the better. One's self-consciousness often has to be ignored. I have frequently said to apprentice speakers and novice preachers, 'Be shameless'. I said this, not to license anything tasteless or inappropriate, but to encourage them not to let natural bashfulness prevent them trying out something imaginative and unexpected.

Projection

One factor which the judges used to look for in our inter-school competitions, and one for which there was a generous apportionment of marks, was 'PROJECTION'. This quality had little to do with projecting the voice. Projecting what, then? The speaker's personality? Not primarily, I hope. I did not pour out my energy explaining, exhorting, encouraging, correcting, demonstrating and wheedling in order to produce a nasty little crop of exhibitionists. Nor did I aim at turning out young men and women skilled in selling themselves to an audience.

I discovered the quality 'projection' when I was eighteen, although I had never heard its technical name. I was a second year novice, and another member of my year asked me to help him prepare his practice sermon. These sermons were preached during supper. Imagine! Our brethren were busy dealing with their sausage and mash or other evening fare; there was a rattle of tea cups, of knives and forks on plates, of serving spoons on platters and the thump of servers' feet as they scurried up and down the refectory. Nobody was looking at you as you preached, except for an occasional glance of curiosity or commiseration. Certainly, nobody wanted you to stampede his emotions or stir his conscience to its depths while he was trying to eat his supper. As a novice I was unaware of the fact that it was in exactly these circumstances, and in that very pulpit at St Beuno's, that Gerard Manley

Hopkins had had to cut his practice sermon short because his fellow students were laughing uncontrollably.

Of all the advice which out of my vast inexperience I gave my colleague, one remark seemed to me the most important at the time. It still does. 'Some of them (our fellow novices) say their sermons into the air, and some of them talk to us. Make sure you don't just say your sermon with us there, but sound as though you are talking to us'. That for me is the essence of projection, to address the congregation, to speak directly to them and not just to deliver a speech in their presence. It is one of the reasons for my dislike of the word-for-word script, that it tempts the preacher to read his/her paper in our presence and not address us. When that happens I feel like shouting out, 'Leave the lectern, leave that piece of paper on it and come down here and talk to us'.

I don't think that I ever used the term 'projection' when I was coaching in school, but I set myself to elicit it as soon as my pupils began to compose actual speeches. I believe that the ground had already been prepared by their experience of having to sing out, 'Mmmaaahhh . . .', trying to hold it for a minute, before 'bouncing it off the far wall'. You cannot give yourself to antics of that sort without stretching the shackles of self-consciousness. Once the youngsters were engaged in rehearsing their speeches I hammered away at them to keep thinking in terms of the audience. 'You must insert your argument into their minds. You want them to see this as you see it; you want them to share your feelings about it'. Some times I had to begin by insisting that they themselves enter more deeply into the material. 'Can you yourself see what you are describing? How do you expect the audience to see and react to it, if you haven't seen it all vividly in your own imagination first?'

By getting them to focus throughout on their subject and on their audience, as well as on the need to present the first to the second as effectively as possible, I hoped to deliver them, at least partially, from that stifling over-awareness of self which we call self-consciousness. Was I trying to blot out their individuality, turning them into mere vehicles for their message? Far from it. When I call on everything I have to deliver my message to this audience, the quality of my thinking, imagination and feelings are openly displayed. What I have to say, and the way I say it will have my own individual stamp. As Buffon, the first anthropologist, rightly remarked, 'Le style, c'est l'homme même'.

In this area the preacher must constantly ask him or herself which is the means and which the end. Am I drawing on my ability to describe arrestingly, to argue convincingly and to entertain − if I have such power − for the sake of the message, or do I regard the message as an opportunity to display my competence as a speaker and the 'gifts' which lie behind it? If I know that I can preach well, or give an interesting and entertaining talk, or that I can charm most of the people who come to see me − an experience I have not myself had − then I must monitor myself carefully. 'He must increase and I must decrease'. 'Projection' is very important. It matters still more that ultimately it is the right Person who is projected.

To Hear Ourselves As Others Hear Us

Under the heading of voice production, I must make mention of the tape recorder. On the subject of amplifiers I was distrustful and disparaging, an attitude based not on a fossilised distaste of modern 'gadgets', but on disillusioning personal experience. About tape recorders on the other hand, I am an enthusiast. They reproduce faithfully enough to make it possible for us to hear ourselves as others hear us, and to evaluate our performance, to rehearse and to experiment. It is a pity if we do not use a tape recorder for each of these purposes. If we cannot find time to experiment and rehearse, we should certainly be able to listen to recordings of our actual performance. People record nuptial masses or masses with a christening. In those cases I can borrow the tape afterwards. Is there any reason why I should not have at least some of my regular sermons recorded? A video recording would be even more helpful. I have watched myself taking part in a discussion, and I have seen myself talking on television, but I have yet to watch myself preach. Should the opportunity arise, I should feel quite apprehensive as to what the camera might show; I should feel even more strongly that

I had no alternative but to face, not the music, but the spectacle.

This chapter has been rather long and involved. To make it easier to assimilate I have drawn up the following summary of its practical contents:

Voice Control

Its principles have their application not only in preaching, but in lecturing, committee work and telephoning ... not to mention conducting the liturgy.

Two Axioms

'Paint your words in large letters on the back wall of the hall'. 'Wherever you happen to be looking, keep thinking in terms of the back row'.

Outline of a training course

STANCE:	Feet firm; grow tall; shoulders back, not taut.
BREATHING:	Push out those lower ribs.
RESONANCE:	Hum powerfully, then 'Mmmaaa ...' Bounce the sound off the opposite wall.
MOUTH OPEN:	'Pretend you're a crocodile'.
ENUNCIATION:	Shape the sound with tongue, teeth and lips, especially the lips.
READING YOUR NOTES:	'Swivel your eyeballs, not lower your head'. Maximum number of words at a glance.
CONTROL OF:	Pitch 'Take a lower note'.

VARIATION OF: Volume
             Pace
             Tone

PAUSES: Paragraphing.

EXPRESSION: Read to children.

SELF-CONSCIOUSNESS: Has to be overridden.

PROJECTION: Talk, not in our presence, but
             to us.

Use the tape recorder, the video if available.

10

'Not The Matter, But The Manner', And The Matter Of Nerves

'I do not much dislike the matter, but the manner of his speech', says Octavius Caesar of a blunt but pertinent intervention by the soldier Enobarbus. Like Octavius, we sometimes find ourselves having to differentiate between someone's manner, which we find disagreeable, and their actions which are quite acceptable. More often our distinction is between the manner and the 'real' person. It is not uncommon to hear such a remark as, 'It's just his manner; he's alright really', or 'Don't be put off by her manner; her heart's in the right place'. We also speak of a telephone manner.

These last few days I have been nagging myself and pestering others about that term 'manner'. We all know what it means, but I have yet to meet anyone who can say what it consists of. It is certainly something on the surface, something quite quickly perceived. Is it something in the field of what we call 'body language' and therefore perceived by the eye alone, or is it a matter of choice of words or of the tone or timbre of the voice? Obviously, a 'telephone manner', good or bad, is registered by the ear alone. Is a pulpit 'manner' a combination of vocabulary, tone of voice and body language?

Manner Resented

It may be difficult to analyse, but Manner is an important factor in the eyes – or ears – of a congregation, and one on which my correspondents hold very definite views. What they dislike most is a 'dogmatic' manner, a term which no-one chose to dissect further. Two people complain of 'being patronised' and a third of being 'talked down to'. A headmaster spoke of a 'distinct air of "I'm in charge"'. The most serious charge, and the most heartfelt, came from a retired surgeon. 'Many preachers sound as though it doesn't matter to them one way or another'.

Manner Commended

Although I have put them first, criticisms of the local clergy on the grounds of their preaching manner were less common than praise. People commented appreciatively on their 'warmth', 'conviction', 'obvious sincerity', 'firmness' and also on the fact that 'they talk with us and not down to us'. Their principal recommendation under the heading of manner was, 'a relaxed and confident manner, which communicates itself to the hearer'. I had the impression reading through this section of my replies that a number of congregations sit through a sermon in real discomfort. They are on edge all the time because of the evident tenseness of the preacher. On the other hand nobody wants a relaxed manner to degenerate into the slovenly. 'Relaxed, but dignified and graceful' is the ideal offered by one person.

After a 'relaxed manner' the second most common appeal was for 'sincerity of manner'. Then came 'firmness', the term frequently going with 'confidence', e.g. 'a firm and confident manner'. Even when they urge firmness and confidence, at least two correspondents warn against that firmness turning into dogmatism. 'Warmth' is another quality often advocated, which I take to be much the same as 'friendliness' and 'caring' in other comments. More than one correspondent made the point that the manner should fit the individual preacher. 'I think the manner of the preacher should fit his character – otherwise there is a strained or false impression'.

I liked the bold metaphor of 'It seems that each individual has got to find out which horse suits his style best and ride that one for all he's worth with confidence'.

I should like to quote two of my replies at greater length. The first was put together by a group of five people:

> 'A firm and expressive manner was desired with a sense of wonder and questioning ... There must be room for individuality and the preacher's own personality to come through with openness of heart and spirit in a friendly manner ... The preacher to be at ease with whatever gives him or her confidence'.

The following comes from a young woman theologically trained and pastorally experienced:

> 'Personally I prefer what might be described as a warm tentativeness ... I want to be befriended by the homilist ... It goes without saying that a homilist should avoid at all costs pomposity, moralising, over-emotionalism. The other very obvious, but crucial point is the variety of modes of manner and expression which are possible and which must be variously chosen and adapted for particular needs and situations. Preaching to 300 young people, for example, is an art in itself, and what will suit them would be utterly inappropriate in an average parish church. It is important that we learn to recognise and develop the particular gifts and style which will best serve the preaching of the word in particular circumstances'.

Scrutinising My Manner

Marx's famous dictum that the important thing is not to understand the world, but to change it, certainly has its application to our preaching manner. I may not be able to define 'manner', but I must be able to change anything defective in my own. I suggest that we begin by examining our underlying attitudes. The priest whose manner is patronising may have allowed his sacerdotal status and the deference it brings to have induced in him a misplaced feeling of superiority. In the pulpit this is reinforced by his literally elevated position with an apparently docile and respectful congregation there below. It is an unpleasant possibility that some of the preachers who 'sound as though it doesn't matter to them one way or the other' have become somewhat jaded and apathetic with regard to this particular duty. God forbid that the same should be true with regard to their pastoral mission in general! Should I become aware of some flaw in my preaching manner, I must humbly, but not obsessively, ask myself whether its roots may not lie in some such deficiency of outlook or motivation.

If I can conscientiously acquit myself on that score, then I must be willing to review my stance, facial expressions, wording and tone of voice. An efficient tape recorder will tell me what I sound like, and enable me to check on my wording. We can be insufficiently sensitive about our words and phrases. I remember trying to persuade a teaching colleague not to say such things as 'I want all the Sixth Form to have a course in Economics', with an emphasis on the 'I want'. I suggested he put his views more impersonally, e.g. 'The Sixth Form would in my opinion benefit from a course in Economics for all'. He was slow to see that beginning with 'I want', and stressing it into the bargain, gave his suggestion a flavour of self-assertion which was more likely to antagonise than persuade.

Tone of voice is a most potent instrument and one to be used circumspectly. It can entirely reverse the import of the words. A compliment such as 'Very interesting!' spoken with a complete absence of enthusiasm, turns into a contemptuous declaration of boredom. Conversely, a criticism or rebuke can be transformed into an endearment. A woman once remarked to me, 'You sometimes say to me, "Don't be a silly girl". It's rather nice'. That was plainly one of the occasions when I got the tone right. When we preach we produce our voices somewhat differently from when we converse. Consequently, there is more likelihood of the tone going wrong and so distorting our meaning, or giving a wrong impression of our attitude. As you speak, monitor not only your words, but your tone. To the same end, always welcome the chance to have yourself recorded.

Unless a cine camera is available, it is not going to be easy to examine your stance, gestures and facial expressions. A full length mirror can be of some help. Perhaps there is one in your wardrobe. I hope that there is one in your sacristy in which you check your vestments before each service. Stand in front of it and take up what I might term your 'speaking position'. Are you standing straight, looking alert, but without tension, 'relaxed but dignified'? Try out the gestures you know you use. Would any of them give an unfavourable impression? This may all prove rather embarrassing, but salutary. As to facial expressions I am at a loss to suggest how you can check these. Addressing the mirror will not I think reproduce the play of your features which occurs as you actually preach. Perhaps you should enlist the help of a candid friend. I can only hope that if our minds and hearts are engaged in what we have to say, and if we are concerned for, and aware of the people to whom we are speaking, then those attitudes will be clearly read in what was called 'my mien'.

The Nightmare Of Nerves

Fortunately, although a congregation may read my countenance, it cannot read my stomach. 'Have you got butterflies in your stomach, Paul?', a sympathetic friend asked, as we neared the Cathedral where I was to preach at the Academic High Mass. 'No', I said, 'It's an anaconda writhing about'. According to my correspondents, congregations want their preachers to look 'relaxed and confident'. How do I look relaxed when I feel more taut than a violin string, when Anathema the Anaconda is doing his aerobics in my guts, and when I know that my knees are about to buckle and my voice die away in a croak? How can I feel confident facing all those people who can see my every movement and hear every tremor in my voice, when I know that my material is not really ready, that what I have to say is uninspired and inadequate, and that I shall undoubtedly at some point lose my way or my mind go blank?

The strange thing is that one can do it. One can feel all these horrors and yet stand there looking, if not nonchalant, reasonably at ease. The human being is capable of quite a remarkable level of concealment. Parents often have to hide their anxieties from their children, lest the children be frightened. As a pastor you will sometimes have to listen to a sad story as though you were hearing it for the first time, when, in truth, you have already heard it in strict confidence from someone else. And, what is more you must not give away the fact that the two accounts in places contradict one-another! I have cited these examples to make the point that concealment and simulation are not necessarily dishonourable. They can be part of our responsibility towards other people. So, when it is time to preach, stand up straight and do your best to give the impression that you have been looking forward to this for a whole week, and intend to relish every minute of it.

Anathema the Anaconda is, if you are interested, still very much alive. He and I have grown old together. Like myself he is much less active, but will try, as I do, to rise to the occasion. The presence of our small, friendly congregation here at St Beuno's seldom incites him to more than a token writhe, but let him sense the special event and the ugly coils are set undulating once again, though with reduced momentum. I have never learned how to expel him or even how to anaesthetise him temporarily. I have usually managed to carry on as though he were not there — rather like that Spartan boy we were told about at school, who gave no sign that there was a wolf concealed beneath his tunic, gnawing at his entrails. Unlike the Spartan boy, I always survived. As for my knees buckling, my voice turning to a croak and I losing the thread and drying up, I will not say that such a debacle never occurred, but rather that it has not happened yet.

Nervousness Beneficial

My anaconda survives, but during the course of our coexistence I have learned to restrict, though not to suspend his activities, by letting certain truths penetrate my mind and imagination. The first of these is that nervousness can actually be a help. When we are nervous, we are more alert, our senses are sharpened, our concentration is enhanced, our reactions are quicker and our energy levels higher. When I am moderately nervous I am a more energetic and effective animal. You may find one day that you are not in the least nervous about preaching to your regular congregation. That is when you should begin to be uneasy. You are probably going to preach less well than in the days when you were on edge beforehand. The snag is of course that excessive nervousness can certainly impair your performance, and we have no emotional thermostat which we can conveniently set at 'Moderate Nervousness'. For the moment let me say no more than that it helps to realise that my nervousness is not some pathological condition, but a transient overdose of an entirely normal, healthy and helpful reaction to my situation.

Nervousness Normal

Nervousness is normal, and universal. We see performers of all kinds, actors, singers and speakers 'up there' on the stage looking wholly at home and at ease. It is obvious to me that they are in their right element, which is why they look so entirely relaxed and natural. I of course don't belong 'up there'. The thought of going on any sort of stage in front of an audience horrifies me. 'I would be far too nervous'. I once had the pleasure of talking to a nationally known entertainer who was to be seen weekly on television. I brought up the subject of nerves.

> 'I have a regular nightmare', she said, 'in which I am on the stage singing, and the audience start making for the exit. I continue to sing my heart out, and they are all leaving'.
> 'Are you ever nervous on the stage?', I asked.
> 'On the first night of any show your legs are made of rubber'.
> 'How long', I persisted, 'have you been going on the stage?'
> 'Since I was nine'.

In quite another setting I was talking to a slightly older woman, an accomplished lecturer and a widely read author. She was highly intelligent, profoundly thoughtful, with a rare talent for relating religious truths to daily life and doing so lucidly and movingly. She made an impressive figure on the platform, her long ebony-black hair framing a strong face with two lustrous dark eyes. She seemed to hold aces in every suit. She certainly belonged 'up there'. That evening we were chatting to kill time before she went in to be one of three lecturers on a panel answering questions arising from the previous week's lectures and discussions. As the evening session drew near the lady started to shiver, not violently, but quite noticeably. I said solicitously, 'It's draughty here. I'll get your coat'. She smiled. 'I'm not cold. This happens every time'.

So remember, as you wait for the service to begin, miserable and out of sorts, plagued by those butterflies or your anaconda, or whatever other creatures have taken up agitated residence in your guts, that you are experiencing what those apparently carefree debonaire professionals have experienced and normally go on experiencing. Nervousness is normal. It may be very nasty and depressingly persistent, but it is still no disqualification. Rather the contrary. A high degree of nervousness is quite compatible with a high level of performance. I wonder whether a complete absence of nerves would be.

Have A Sense Of Proportion

One summer I was asked, almost at the last minute, to give an eight days retreat at a certain convent. I agreed, but with much apprehension. That particular congregation always had retreat givers of distinction, novicemasters, theology lecturers and the like. I, an obscure schoolmaster, had been suddenly asked because the appointed director had fallen ill. He had a Doctorate in Ascetical Theology and had founded a magazine dealing with the subject. I was stepping into shoes several sizes too large for me. How could I provide for retreatants used to such four star spiritual catering? Comforting myself with the thought that so late in the season they had to have me or nobody, I went and did my best.

I gave the retreat according to the formula of a 'preached' retreat of that era, three talks each day and a homily at mass. Being still very interested in schools I found some time to look at the school in which the community taught. The Headmistress was kind enough to spend an afternoon showing me round the buildings and later, during part of an evening, showed me proudly over her labs. She remarked, to my pleasure, that it was interesting to have a retreat from someone who also worked in a school.

Seven years later I was lecturing at a Theology Conference, and glimpsed among those attending it, a nun whose face I knew I had seen before, but could not remember when or where. The next day it came to me. She was the Headmistress in that teaching community about which I had been so apprehensive. I introduced myself to her and she looked at me without recognition. Well, it had taken me a day to place her, so I allowed another twenty-four hours and approached her again. She still had no recollection whatever of me or the retreat.

'But you showed me over your school'.
'I'm afraid I don't remember'.

I was a little nettled, and started to demonstrate how well I remembered her.

'You read ...', and I named her university subject.
'Yes, that's right'.
'At X University'.
'Yes, I did ... but I don't have the memory of a Jesuit'.

That lady did me a great deal of good. I had been nervous of that retreat. I had worked hard on it, preparing my talks and interviewing people between whiles. Sister Headmistress had sat through a minimum of thirty-two carefully thought out, carefully delivered addresses. Seven years later she could not remember a thing about the retreat or even, after firm prompting, recognise my face or my name. How very liberating! I never worried about a preached retreat again. I worked equally hard on them, but with far less anxiety.

I have told this story, long though it is, because it encapsulates for me an important lesson. Much nervousness is generated by our exaggerated notion of the amount of notice other people take of us. I stand up to preach very much on edge because everyone can see my every movement and hear, I hope, every sound I make. But are they really going to watch me so closely throughout? Are they really going to listen with the concentration of a sound engineer monitoring his equipment? I should be so lucky! Those few minutes on a Sunday are for me charged with emotion as I pray that I will succeed, and miserably fear that I shall fail. Not so for the congregation. Of course they prefer getting an interesting sermon competently delivered to sitting through a dull, halting one. Yet my sermon and I occupy a small part of their mental universe somewhere towards its periphery, while filling a large central area of my own. That Headmistress' total non-recognition of me took me abruptly into her world where I did not even exist. When the shock to my vanity had passed, I felt airborne with a sense of my own insignificance.

You may ask if this incident proved such effective anti-anaconda therapy in the area of retreats, why was it less so with regard to preaching sermons. In fact, the experience did help in that department too. The snag has been that so often when preaching I have felt myself to be carrying a reputation other than my own. As a teacher, when I went into a local parish I was a 'Jesuit from St X College', and was going to bring credit, or less than credit, to the Society and, which was of more immediate importance, to the school. At Oxford I was not Paul Edwards, but the Master of Campion Hall, and had always to think of my 'house' and its members. The latter were always pleased to hear, 'Your Master preached a good sermon'. If they sometimes heard the opposite they tactfully kept the fact to themselves. From time to time I have preached in a non-Roman Catholic church or chapel. There I was very anxious not to fall beneath the usually higher standards of other denominations. I hope that my anxieties were for the Society, the School, the Hall or the Roman Church and were not, under cover of these very respectable pretexts, rooted in egotism.

And A Little Humility

'Humility is endless', says T S Eliot in 'East Coker'. It brings, I firmly believe, endless blessings, one of which is a diminished nervousness. The more concerned I am to make an impression, the more it matters to me to receive admiration and applause the greater will be my fear of failure. Happy the man or woman who has no need to make a great impression; they shall have less fear. Akin to humility, and perhaps a subdivision of it, is what I call un-self-centredness, i.e. a concentration on the message I want to deliver and the people to whom I am trying to deliver it, which makes me oblivious of myself. I may remain very anxious as to whether the message is going to be effectively conveyed, but somehow this outward-directed concern handicaps one's delivery less than a morbid preoccupation with what they will think of me.

And Practise Hard

The most helpful dictum I ever heard on the subject of nervousness came to me from a lecturer in dentistry. When she herself had been a timid, if promising, student, her instructor in surgical techniques reassured her with the aphorism, 'Confidence comes with competence, and competence comes with practice'.

Practice, I have come to believe, never lets you down. I would divide practice into:

TRAINING: by which I mean not so much instruction, as regular exercise or regular drill in the basic skills.

REHEARSAL: i.e. 'dry runs' of parts, or of the whole, for some specific occasion.

EXPERIENCE: a factor I need not define.

When my pupils stood up to deliver their first public speeches they stood up straight, they breathed deeply, they opened their mouths fully. They had done these things regularly in their training and their rehearsals, and did them automatically. However, their nervousness still marred their 'projection' and interfered with their control of the pauses. The principal casualty was their 'paragraphing'. They lacked the third ingredient, experience, which is usually necessary to acquire mastery of tone and pace and the delicate art of the pause. And it is only the most extrovert who can 'project' a speech first time.

The training which the clergy receive in the basic skills of voice control seems to vary greatly. Rehearsal is usually a luxury beyond the reach of most of us. Experience on the other hand, comes to us all. The dividends of experience come faster and larger, the more *aware* I am of the techniques I must learn to master, the more *alert* I am to my own deficiencies in those techniques, the *keener* I am to correct those weaknesses.

All my well-founded observations on this subject of nerves may give you no comfort whatever as your first sermon looms and you wish that the end of the world would come first. You will survive to preach again, and to be nervous again. It may all seem a vicious circle of jitters, performance, relief. It is actually an ascending spiral which will carry you into the ranks of the experienced and, I hope, highly competent preachers.

11

'Can These Bones Live?'

At one period of my life my preparation for the Sunday sermon included two elements not mentioned in the chapter, 'Preparation De Luxe'. On Saturday evening I would settle down to read some lyric poetry and then to watch 'Match Of The Day'. I read the poetry because it struck deep into the soil of my mind, reached the roots of my imagination and stirred my emotions. The poets also reminded me how effective words can be, how vividly they can present our thoughts and feelings, how deeply they can move us. The poems, I believe, 'tuned' my ear, making it more sensitive as I sought the right word, the right phrase, and worked to weave both into smoothly running sentences.

And 'Match Of The Day'? I watched the football for its raw vitality. I steeped myself in the vigour of the players, not merely their physical vigour, but in the passionate determination with which they fought for the ball, and their total dedication to placing it between those three sticks at the opposite end of the field. Superb physical stamina, intense athletic training, refined footballing skills, tactical flair and years of experience were all brought together and focused exclusively on the movement of that ball to the right place at the right moment, as though it were the one thing that mattered in the world. Was I, I would ask myself, bringing a tithe of that vigour, skill and dedication to the job of carrying the word of God to the next day's congregation? How casual, how amateur, how feeble I would look in comparison with any of those twenty-two men battling to put that leather ball into the right net.

Then the crowd! What a mistake it is to think of football spectators as passive. The involvement of the supporters was often as obvious as that of the players, and more raucous, volatile and impatient. You could feel the will of the crowd trying to propel their side to the opposing goalmouth; their frustration when a promising chance was missed; their alarm when their own goal was under attack. Watching, listening and feeling even through the television screen the pulsating passion of those supporters, I would think of the next day's congregation. They were a good congregation, willing to listen to a longish explanation, quick to laugh at my lighter asides and sometimes saying an appreciative word afterwards. Yet the contrast with Anfield or Old Trafford (I am an Evertonian, but that was a depressing period at Goodison) was so conspicuous. As the match ended and Jimmy Hill came on to pass judgement, I did not dream of being the Johann Cruyff of preaching, or of so moving a congregation that I would have to perform a lap of honour round the chapel. I did however feel stimulated, even nagged, to instil all the life I could into the next day's sermon.

Breathing Life Into The Sermon

In Chapter 7 I spoke of the 'skeletal structure' of the sermon, and in Chapter 8 of 'fleshing out' that structure with words, phrases and illustrations. Into the resulting composite I must infuse all the life I can. Were I asked to define 'life' in this context, I should not be able to offer a Cartesian 'clear and distinct idea' in reply. Yet that fact worries me not at all. We all respond to its stimulating presence or feel its depressing absence in the performance of a play, the rendering of a piece of music, in a game, a lecture or a sermon. Below I list the factors which seem to me to give a sermon 'life'.

Commitment

The first ingredient, I believe, is the COMMITMENT of the preacher. Remember my footballers. They train regularly and they put into a match every ounce of energy and all their skill. I ought to engage every relevant faculty in my preparation of a sermon; my background knowledge, my ability to acquire new knowledge, my experience, my imagination, my inventiveness and my feelings. Again, in the delivery I should 'give it all I have'. This does not mean shouting or melodramatic changes of voice or extravagant gestures. It has more to do with accurate control; with keeping my ear sensitively tuned to my voice and my eye keenly observant of the reactions of the congregation. Try not to let it sound laboured. The most effective preparation and the ideal delivery will make everything sound effortless. Get anywhere near that standard and somebody will say, 'You have a great gift!'

The Personal

Commitment does not just mean pouring out my energy; it means engaging my whole self as far as is relevant. All preaching should be PERSONAL. I may have taken much of my material from the commentaries, but I make it my own. I must have digested the information and the observations, used my imagination on them, and, if the subject calls for it, 'felt' the scene and its import. For example, if I am preparing a homily on The Storm On The Lake and have read a description of the sudden storms which erupt on the Sea of Galilee, I must do my best to visualise the event. If the commentaries point to God's control of wind and water in the Creation story, in the Flood narrative, and in the Passage Through The Red Sea, then I must make myself feel the deep awe behind 'Who, then, is this, that even the wind and the sea obey him?'

You may have heard the cynical comment that higher education is a process by which information passes from the notebook of the lecturer to the notebook of the student without passing through the head of either. It must never be the case with our preaching that the matter of a sermon has been taken from our Theology notes, or from some handy book and simply passed on to the congregation, as though we were shop assistants taking something off the shelves and handing it over the counter. We should for instance find our own words and our own comparisons. We must be somewhat like those creatures who find food, eat it and then regurgitate it in more digestible form for their young.

When I say that our preaching should be personal, we are back with the problem I raised in Chapter 3. Some of my correspondents asked for personal reminiscences from the preacher, while others expressed a strong repugnance. I myself use them because they seem to me to arouse interest, and to make my point more vividly. What matters is where my focus is. If I use the story of The Storm On The Lake as an opportunity to give a long account of what happened to me in a small boat off the West of Ireland, then I shall have taken most of the spotlight. If I use such an experience to help the congregation to enter into the fright of the disciples and their consequent awe at the storm's stilling, then I have helped them to focus on the gospel, which is why I am there. My story must be a stepping stone to Christ's story, and a stepping stone is quickly left behind.

I myself believe that personal reminiscence is useful precisely because it is personal, and also because it is concrete. It is something which I can describe the better because it is mine. It must, however, be handled with discretion. It must always be a stepping stone, and never become a road block; and there are other snags which I must circumvent, especially the following pair:

In the days when parish 'missions' were a regular and dramatic part of parish life, the Jesuit in charge of that apostolate was giving a group of newly ordained Jesuits a series of talks on the subject. He devoted one talk to the manifold difficulties which arise during a mission. He illustrated each of them with a story of how he himself had encountered that particular problem, and had deftly and diplomatically produced an ideal solution. At the end of his talk he asked if there were questions. Immediately a hand went up. 'Please, Father', enquired a soft, cultivated voice with the merest hint of irony, 'To what do you ascribe your unvarying success?' We must avoid sounding like that unfortunate missioner. Looking back through the pages of this book, I wonder whether I have sometimes exposed myself to the same barbed question. I don't think that I have ever done so when preaching.

To go to the other extreme to chronicle my failure is, pace the lady who said that she could learn more from my failures than my successes, equally inappropriate. A congregation does not want to listen to its spiritual guide forever harping on his own ineptitude. Nor do they want him to turn into an amateur entertainer, telling comic stories at his own expense. You are a priest or deacon discharging a ministerial role where Christians are gathered for worship, and you must not compromise the essential dignity of the office or of the occasion. Not that dignity is the same thing as pomposity, or requires you to maintain an unbroken solemnity. There is room for humour and, I believe, a little gentle self-depreciation, as long as they serve, and are seen by the congregation to serve, in a quite subordinate way, our wholly serious purpose of presenting a living gospel.

Be Concrete

At one period, if I was giving a preached retreat I always held a session of shared prayer in the late evening. We took a gospel passage, reflected on it, shared our reflections, prayed silently over them and finally shared something of our prayer. In one retreat the sessions flowed very easily and very rewardingly. At first I chose the gospel passage, but according to the dictum, 'It is the function of the teacher to eliminate himself', I soon handed over to some volunteer. One evening someone chose The Woman Taken In Adultery and the session was particularly moving. The next evening a very learned Scandinavian nun chose a very different section of St John, I cannot remember exactly which. I do remember that it was replete with those profound Johannine concepts 'truth', 'life', 'glory' etc. The session proved very laborious. In contrast with The Woman Taken In Adultery this passage had no narrative, no dialogue, no interplay of character, nothing that one could mentally visualise. There were few reflections offered, and even those sounded a little forced. The erudite lady herself obviously moved with complete ease among abstractions, and had no sense at all that most other minds cry out for the concrete, the particular, the imaginable.

Life is not abstract. Neither should our preaching be. We have to deal with eternal truths, but we must express them in *concrete* terms. I have already cited the dissatisfaction of the experienced teacher with a sermon on charity with 'abstract noun piled upon abstract noun'. Most people, like the members of my prayer group, need to imagine things. To have concrete illustrations they can visualise, and unlike that group of nuns, are usually unwilling to persevere without them. The Fourth Gospel does contain the abstract nouns I mentioned in the last paragraph. It also has stories as vivid, as dramatic, and moving as anything in the Synoptics, e.g. The Woman At The Well, The Man Born Blind, The Raising Of Lazarus. The Johannine Christ describes his mission in brief, unforgettable, metaphors, 'I am the good shepherd', 'I am the true vine', 'I am the light of the world'. On occasion he makes his point by providing an abundance of wine or of bread and fish, a very concrete demonstration of his role. In the Synoptic gospels Christ makes much use of stories, one of a particularly vicious mugging on the Jericho road, and another of a redundant manager sweetening possible employers with backhanders. Others are drawn from ordinary events in agriculture, fishing or commercial dealing. His briefer illustrations are taken from the same familiar background, largely rural, sometimes urban, frequently domestic. Almost everything he says evokes a vivid mental picture, easily imaginable, very memorable, not always pleasant (e.g. 'it would be better for him if a great millstone were hung round his neck and he were thrown into the sea'). Every preacher should take Christ's teaching skills as a model. It is for us to express Christian doctrine in clear pictures, in lively comparisons, in stories (brief ones), through examples, in clear down to earth terms. For most of us this is hard work. It is much easier to rabbit on about 'charity', 'modern materialism' or any other tired abstraction.

About ten years ago I went to a lecture on 'The Church And The Churches' given by a conspicuously 'promising' young cleric from the Apostolic Nunciature. In the course of his talk the speaker mentioned a total of five people, of whom I still remember three, St Peter, St Augustine and the Holy Spirit. There was no reference at all to any historical event, to any historical situation, to any example, real or imaginary, of the principles he was enunciating. He built for us an elegant construction of shimmering ecclesiological concepts in a dimension quite unconnected with Planet Earth, where the two-legged inhabitants quarrel and blunder, love and lust, yearn for a better world and too often make a mess of the one they have.

Come question time, I protested somewhat vehemently. True to his training, the fledgling diplomat listened to me with polite interest, remained perfectly unperturbed by my strictures and answered none of them, except to say that he thought five a perfectly adequate number of individuals to mention. I would not, I think, have minded so much if the young man had not plainly been destined to represent at a high level the Church which he had just treated in such an unreal fashion. Perhaps I owe him some gratitude for a memorable demonstration of how we should never preach, never lecture, never even talk, except in a purely academic discussion with the highly cerebral.

Be Topical

One way to avoid 'timeless' treatment of a subject is to introduce something topical. What we have to say will have a better chance of sounding 'living', if we apply it to an up-to-date situation. Not that I am recommending for your congregation a steady diet of President Clinton, 'Gazza' and Madonna. Like St Matthew's scribe 'trained for the Kingdom of Heaven' we should bring out by way of illustration 'what is new and what is old'. Living things do have both a past and a present, and neither aspect should be missing from our own religious thinking and practice, or from our preaching. The last can often benefit from a touch of the totally up-to-date, i.e. the events of the last twenty-four hours. I have used something seen on TV on Saturday night in a Sunday morning homily, and preaching at an evening mass during a Theology course, I have found it helpful to make some reference – not a forced one – to something said at one of the morning lectures.

One year Guy Fawkes Night was being celebrated on a Saturday night when the first reading at the Sunday Mass was the story of Moses and the Burning Bush. I felt that this coincidence had to be exploited. That evening I stalked through the streets of our neighbourhood in the company of a young woman with a first class degree in psychology. We walked from bonfire to bonfire, sometimes stopping to watch from a distance the tall flames leaping higher than the rooftops, sometimes getting as close as we could to the blaze to stare into its 'gold vermilion' centre. We discussed the experience over a late cup of tea, and then I stayed up beyond midnight, asking myself in the remembered light of those bonfires what I could learn about the Deity from the fact that fire is so frequently a symbol of His presence. Next day my congregation had a 'morning after Bonfire Night' exposition of the Burning Bush. The merit, in my view, of such topicality is that one's material has not been, and is clearly seen not to have been, lifted down from some dusty shelf in one's mind, but to have been freshly worked out. I am offering the congregation not my dead knowledge, but my living thinking.

Freshness

Such thinking is fresh thinking, and I suppose topicality is really a sub-division of FRESHNESS, which is the next heading in my list of things helping to give life to a sermon. Our preaching should be as fresh as we have the time, energy and wit to make it. Can I come at the subject from an unexpected angle? I think that I managed such a fresh approach with my Bonfire Sermon and on the occasion when I expounded 'Thou art Peter . . .' in terms of a visit to Stonehenge the previous afternoon. Such opportunities may be comparatively rare, but we should always be on the alert to spot them and exploit them.

It is easier, but quite hard work all the same, to think of new illustrations and fresh phrases. Begin by recoiling from 'time honoured' formulae and clichés. At this point I remember my mother's reaction to a priest who used to hold forth with great unction on the Sacrifice of the Holy Mass. ''Olocausts and 'ole burnt offerings!' she said caustically, 'What do I know about 'olocausts and 'ole burnt offerings?' For that undoubtedly devout priest that formula had become some sort of rhetorical incantation. Elsewhere I mentioned the priest whose every sermon included at some point the words 'the warp and woof' of our faith. Like an engineer scrutinising structures on which lives depend for the least sign of metal fatigue, examine your every discourse for 'word fatigue', and be ready to look for a new component.

To have some degree of freshness a thing does not have to be brand new. Bread just out of the oven may have been made to a traditional formula, but it is freshly baked. If a sermon comes out of real thinking and genuine feeling, even if the thoughts and phrases are largely traditional, there will still be a degree of freshness about it. One reason why I always try to keep my address stirring in my mind right up to the moment of delivery is to give it, I hope, something of that 'straight-out-of-the-oven' flavour.

Humour

Lastly I come to a factor I have hitherto shirked from discussing – humour. Of humour I wrote some years ago:

> Humour is no trivial element in our lives. It is a prerogative of man [nowadays, having learned better I would say 'humanity'] which the brute creation does not share. It springs from our intelligence, imagination and creativity. It eases tension, defuses hostility, creates rapport between individuals, and enriches friendship. It makes the unpleasant a little more tolerable and renders the agreeable even more enjoyable. It also provides an effective test of the genuine. True dignity and real worth can tolerate being made fun of; portentousness never.

My views have not changed. I still see humour as a God-given element, genial, versatile, and enriching, for which there is no substitute. Nevertheless, I have been reluctant to discuss it for two reasons. My first reason is that humour, like free will, seems to lie right outside our ordinary categories, and so defies analysis. Theorising about either is rather like trying to illustrate colours with black and white photographs. My other problem is that the entire New Testament seems to have been composed without a shred of humour, the Holy Spirit and His human collaborators evidently not sharing my view about its multiform benefits and irreplaceable value.

Here I need to remind myself how ruthlessly economical the

gospel writers had to be. The Fourth Gospel says that were all Jesus' deeds to be written up 'the world itself would not contain the books that would be written'. Yet the four gospels put together occupy in my edition of the R.S.V. less than 111 pages. Where so many events, and presumably even more sayings, had to go unrecorded there was certainly no space for Jesus' jokes. Actually, I believe that there are traces of his humour in the parables and in the nickname he gave to James and John. (Did he have nicknames for the others?) I also think that I can detect an element of teasing sometimes when he is putting questions to the Twelve. I certainly cannot believe that so gifted, so imaginative, so sensitive a man did not have a highly developed sense of humour, or that so dedicated and resourceful an educator could neglect such a valuable teaching aid. I would argue in the same way with regard to the unrelievedly serious letters of St Paul. Long as some of these letters are, they are still crammed almost to bursting point with instruction, advice and exhortation. Space and parchment were too precious for anything less urgent. Again I cannot credit that someone able to handle such a variety of stops, was without that important stop on his keyboard, or lacked the ability to play it when it served his purpose.

I also need to take into consideration the volatility of humour which makes it very difficult to transmit. Humour for the most part belongs to the here and now, to this situation, and depends on a sympathetic resonance between the narrator and his audience. Taken out of context it evaporates. It may not survive translation from one language to another. It is even less likely to survive a change of culture. So perhaps the Holy Spirit judged wisely when He decided to edit out of the record of Christ's preaching the highly perishable element of humour.

We likewise need to make shrewd judgements about the use of humour. It must always be seen to serve the serious business of putting across a serious message. I heard it said of a very gifted preacher that he preached in Westminster Cathedral on the Last Judgement and 'brought the roof down'. Few if any of the people who left the Cathedral having laughed heartily and often, walked away without a sobering reflection on what it might be like, in the preacher's words, 'to have left this earth and to find oneself without the shadow of an earthly excuse'. Our humour must not be a distraction, nor must it jar with the message or the liturgical setting or the expectations of the congregation. The principle of 'this congregation on this occasion' is never more relevant than when we are assessing the possibilities of introducing the light touch.

Please don't let my caution frighten you off. Humour is much too enriching an ingredient, too valuable an aid to digestion even of spiritual truths, to be dropped from every one of your menus. So experiment discreetly just as a cook does with seasoning. Never take refuge from the creative effort involved, or from the risk of failure and embarrassment by pleading that 'Humour must come naturally'. As I have argued before, is it natural to swim or to ride a bicycle? Your first efforts at humour may be as desperate as your first attempts to keep afloat, or as clumsy as your first struggles to stay upright on two wheels. Persevere! You may uncover quite a rich vein of humour as several of my apprentice speakers did. The chances are that you will achieve at least competence in this respect as in others.

The first article I was asked to write was on 'Christian Joy'. It was consistently solemn, heavy and in places turgid. For my seventh article I was given the title 'Despair'. Soon after its publication a Reverend Mother, who was a lecturer in a College of Education, told me that as she read it she kept bursting into guffaws. Between my first and seventh articles I had discovered my own lode of humour-bearing ore and become moderately adept at exploiting it. If there are few nuggets of humour to be found in this book, it is because their production, as with any skill, requires constant practice. A 'Spiritual Exercises Centre' does not, I find, offer a wealth of opportunities.

Let Live!

Finally, I should like to suggest that life, or the lack of it, is in every aspect of our preaching:

in our STANCE:	which is another reason why we must not sag against the lectern, or if we are seated, slump in the chair.
in our GESTURES:	which, even if slow, should look controlled rather than feeble.
in our TONE of VOICE:	which does not have to be loud. A quiet voice can thrill no less than a resonant challenging one.
in the PACE of our delivery:	which should never drag. I am not saying that our delivery has to be rapid. When Ronnie Corbett or Johnnie Carson tell a story their delivery in words per minute is quite slow, yet you could never say that their narrative drags. They are grandmasters in the art of the pause and the change of pace.

Ultimately, vitality in a sermon is always rooted in the *mind and heart of the preacher*. Our preaching will never be dead if our thinking and our personal commitment are living things, and if we have a springiness of mind and also a real warmth in our hearts towards the gospel message and those to whom we are preaching.

12

At Length

'Who is it this week?', the children wanted to know as their mother herded them to the car on Sunday morning.

'Father Paul', she replied, correctly interpreting their 'it' to refer to the celebrating priest, or more importantly the preacher.

The boy, a youth of fourteen, scowled and his eleven-year old sister grimaced. 'He preaches for a long time', they complained.

'Yes', their mother conceded, adding placatingly, 'But it will be good'.

The children remained unreconciled. 'Better', declared the lad morosely, 'a short, bad sermon than a long good one'.

On the subject of a sermon's length most of my correspondents had views almost as uncompromising as that of young James, the lad in the above story. There is quite a lobby for short sermons. The extreme: 'Our curate at midweek masses preaches a brilliant sermon (1½ mins.) Excellent five minute sermon on Sundays. After that I sleep'. Similarly: 'People have audio memories of only a few minutes. This is a fact and there is no point in moralising about it. Therefore not more than five minutes'. A little more flexible: 'Brevity is high on my list of qualities. Five minutes is about right, ten is stretching it and fifteen grave matter'. I wonder if there is any significance in the fact that all three replies came from men who taught with me over several years and heard me preach on a number of occasions?

Other correspondents allow a little longer. A lay pastoral worker: 'I prefer short homilies, 5–8 minutes.' She goes on to

140

add a qualification made by others: 'But if it is good, I don't mind if it is 15 – 20 minutes'. A similar point of view: 'It takes a good man to captivate his audience for more than ten minutes at a stretch'. A minority of my replies suggest an optimum of '10 – 12 minutes or even 12 – 15'. Anglicans for the most part allowed their preachers a longer time, especially at the evening service. However, it was an American Catholic, resident in Ireland, who replied, '13 – 15 mins. at mass, not less or I won't think it important, 25 – 28 at a mission'.

For a few length was irrelevant if the sermon were worthwhile. A headmaster wrote, 'Length is only tedious when the preacher is incompetent'. A surgeon states, 'I can listen to one speaker with rapt attention for an hour, while with another I am bored in ten minutes'. Curiously enough that lady is a close friend of James's mother, but I do not suppose that James and she discuss their diametrically opposed criteria for evaluating sermons. I liked the comment of one group reply, 'The preacher should be able to sense when he is losing the attention of his audience'. I warmed particularly to the telegraphese of a biology teacher: 'Length – judge it from the reaction of the congregation – heads up – rustle of papers – may be even clues from a friend in the congregation'. She can obviously read the signals of inattention in a class and expects a similar awareness in a preacher. Personally, I do not think that I would want a pal in the congregation to wave his missalette, or to pull his left ear when he thought I had reached my 'sell by date', but we should welcome comment after the service on any aspect of the sermon including its length.

Where does this multiplicity of opinions leave us? What are you to do when some people regard five minutes as a maximum, others expect longer and one lady thinks that anything under 13 minutes means that your subject is unimportant? I myself fall back on my overriding formula 'this congregation on this occasion', together with my judgement as a teacher. I do not claim that I always get it right. I suspect that as my hair has whitened my average sermon has grown longer, thus earning the disapproval of James and his sister.

At a weekday mass in a parish church I would regard three

minutes as exactly right. On Sunday morning I would find five minutes too little, because it seems to me that you have to gather the attention of a Sunday morning congregation and lead them into your subject. That done, five minutes on the real meat of your sermon might suffice. The atmosphere of a Sunday evening mass always seems to me a little more leisurely, a little more relaxed and I was prepared to speak for a little longer. At a university chaplaincy I spoke longer again, because I judged that people who were habituated to an hour's lecture were certainly capable of listening and following for as long as eighteen minutes. Mind you, I worked hard to make every sentence worth listening to. I tried to give them full value in return for their time.

The special occasions, the Nuptial Mass, the Golden Jubilee of Sister N., the funeral, the Annual Mass for the Catholic Teachers Federation have each to be appraised individually. They present the same problem. I must not by too brief an address appear to underrate the importance of the event, and yet neither a nervous bridal couple nor a bereaved family want to sit through a long harangue, while Sister N. and the teachers, having arranged hymns and bidding prayers, are equally anxious that you should not go on too long. The problem is the same, but the solution has to be individual. As in most circumstances experience and knowledge of the people involved helps. We should never hesitate to ask advice. Ask someone who appreciates your difficulty, knows the people involved and uses figures precisely, i.e. a person for whom 'five minutes' means approximately 300 seconds, and not the Celtic 'five minutes', the relationship of which to actual measured time I have never been able to fathom.

Several parish churches manned by Jesuits in Victorian times have at the back of the church a large clock, which neither the worshipping congregation, nor the celebrant in the days when he had his back to the congregation, could see. Obviously, the clock had but one purpose. To confront the preacher throughout his sermon with the steady, inexorable march of its minute hand. Victorian Jesuits with their solemn, often melodramatic discourses did not subscribe to young James's view of preaching. They would nevertheless have agreed with him that the passage of time is an important factor, and quite literally, one never to be lost sight of by the preacher. I miss those clocks. I have tried putting my watch on the lectern, but that means removing the lectionary and staying at the lectern. On top of that, the ledge on the lectern is often so narrow that the watch is not at all safe on it. So I have to remain sensitively alert to the passing of time without the benefit of an external check. This is not an area in which I can claim 'unvarying success'.

Is there any way of calculating the length of your projected homily beforehand? I have on occasion been taken aback by the unjustified confidence with which someone preparing a first homily will say to me, 'It will only take seven or eight minutes', when it is perfectly clear to me from the elaborate plan which they have just outlined that it is more likely to take twenty-five. I know only of one way for the beginner to calculate with any accuracy the likely duration of an address. It is to write out the piece in full, count the words quite accurately, leaving out the indefinite article 'a' (I don't know why) and allow a minute for every hundred words. That is approximately the right speed of delivery for a full size church. In a smaller chapel you can go a little faster.

You may object that people speak at different speeds, and that some people use longer words than others, which must surely affect their rate of delivery. I admit the force of both objections and find them unanswerable. I can only affirm that in years of coaching debaters and public speaking competitors, all of whom had to keep strictly within the allotted time, this very arbitrary rule of thumb worked with surprising efficiency. Two very effective speakers were slower still, averaging just over 90 words a minute, but they stand out as exceptions. What will not help, is to read your script slowly — as you think — at your desk with a watch in front of you. You will be reading at twice or three times the speed needed in a largish place.

There is a worse snag. I have done my best to persuade you not to write the homily in full, but to be content with notes. How, then, are you to calculate the length? In fact, as I admitted in the original context, I have seldom succeeded in persuading first-time preachers not to compose a complete written text. In that case they may as well use it to estimate the delivery time. What about the first-timer who is courageous enough to accept my challenge and prepare only notes? He or she must keep very careful control of the amount of material which goes into the projected address, stoutly resisting the novice's itch to stuff it with every thought they can come up with. A single point, when it has been introduced, briefly explained, economically developed, sparingly applied and then concisely concluded, will be both long enough and short enough. Keep to such an uncomplicated scheme during your early sermons; refuse to be drawn into elaboration, and then, as your experience accumulates, you will find yourself able to gauge, if only roughly, the relationship between material and delivery time.

Your growing experience should also bring you a sense of the congregation; of whether they are still interested, or becoming inattentive and weary. If you are indeed losing them, is it because you are being dull or because you are speaking for too long? If the former, then you may woo them with a brighter tone, a livelier manner and a brisker pace. If, however, you are losing attention because you are going on too long, then have the common sense and the decisiveness to curtail your matter ruthlessly. There is no need whatever to go through all the examples you thought of, or all the applications you have worked out. Your address is not a work of art which it would be a sacrilege to mutilate. You are there to feed that congregation, and if it turns out that you have prepared too big a meal, then keep some of it for another occasion. If it is suitable only for this occasion and will not keep, then throw it out. It is we who must pay the price for our mistakes, and not our congregation.

The Two Thirds Rule

The mother of one of my most responsive debaters used to be amused by the meticulous care with which the lad pored over his notes, trying to calculate at which word occurred the 'two thirds point'. He had been introduced to the very important 'Two Thirds Rule' by Fr Anthony Horan S.J., a colleague of mine over several years and a shrewd debating coach. Tony would enunciate this 'never-to-be-forgotten' rule as follows:

> The attention of any audience listening to any talk, whether it be a three minute speech or an hour's lecture, will begin to fall away with one third of the address still to come. Therefore any speech or sermon, no matter how long or short, must at about the two-thirds point have something to revive their interest. It may be a joke, a vivid illustration, an unexpected twist in the argument, anything relevant which will recall their attention to its previous level.

My own version would put equal stress on the attitude of the speaker:

> Two thirds the way through any sermon, speech etc., with the midpoint clearly past and the ending now on the horizon, the concentration of both speaker and audience tends to slacken. The speaker, to compensate for this, must deliberately gather himself, and by some phrase, touch of humour or unexpected gambit, rally the listeners and lead them on with revived interest into the final third.

The 'Two Thirds Rule' passed from Tony's technical vocabulary into mine, and 'paragraphing' from mine into his.

As I was composing the above statement of the rule another part of my mind presented me with an uncomfortable question. Does that rule apply to the written word as well as to the spoken? Should a book, and each chapter in a book, receive a deliberate infusion of 'brightening' material two thirds the way through? Would an experienced communicator have automatically furnished it? I have been nervously scrutinising the structure of this book and some of its individual chapters, calculating the approximate 'two thirds point' and assessing how interesting my material was. You see, I do listen to myself, even when it is the written, and not the spoken word which I am presenting to others.

Keeping Fit

Sportsmen and athletes do not spend the whole of every training session practising only those skills which they deploy on the pitch or track. They have to develop and maintain an all round physical fitness. I remember that in the days when Test cricketers travelled to Australia by ship, a well known athlete was appointed to keep the team 'fit' during the voyage, and to present them in tip-top physical condition for the start of their tour. He did not, it is said, endear himself to the players by requiring them to run − we did not yet use the term 'jog' − umpteen times round the deck in the early morning. I hope that I shall incur less odium with my suggestions as to how the preacher can develop and maintain a 'background fitness' to reinforce the special skills described in earlier chapters.

Exercise 1. *Listen, watch and judge*

The first exercise I would recommend is that you listen to and watch speakers of every sort and on a variety of occasions, preachers, politicians, lecturers, the Chairman of the Governors on Prize Night and newscasters. The newscasters are first class professionals. They enunciate excellently, delivering their words quite quickly, yet perfectly clearly, and seeming to do so quite naturally and effortlessly. They also have an admirable control of their tone of voice, deftly adapting it item by item; a touch of solemnity for a disaster, of regret over the latest unemployment figures, of brisk interest in the sports results. As for the other categories of speakers, never be satisfied with merely listening and watching. Judge and analyse. Was the sermon/speech a success? What were its good qualities? What in your opinion did it lack? Force yourself to formulate a verdict and be able to justify it in detail. If someone asks what you thought of the sermon/speech, by all means give them a brief reply, and spare them a technical dissection. But do not spare yourself. Question yourself along the following lines:

STANCE: Dignified? Relaxed?
                     Appropriate?

MANNER: Relaxed? Warm? Sincere?
                     Respectful to the hearers?
                     Appropriate to the occasion?

MATTER:	Factually accurate? Worth saying? Of use to this congregation? (of a sermon) Persuasive?
DEVELOPMENT:	Logical? Well explained? Well illustrated? Well applied? Originality? Freshness of treatment?
INTRODUCTION AND CONCLUSION: VOICE:	Brief? Appropriate? Effective? Easily audible? Clearly enunciated? Pleasant? Flexible? Variety of tone, pace and inflection reinforcing development?
STYLE:	Lucid? Vocabulary appropriate? Phrasing graceful? Lively? Fitting the speaker?
PROJECTION:	Did the preacher/speaker address the audience or did he or she give a talk in their presence?
HUMOUR:	Was there any? Was it in good taste? Effective or irrelevant?
GESTURE:	Natural? Varied? Effectively reinforcing the words?
LENGTH:	Well judged? The two thirds rule?

Does my questionnaire seem an over-elaborate instrument to use on a short homily or the 'few words' of the Deputy Mayor at the opening of the new Senior Citizens Club? I should like you to be in the habit of assessing every bit of preaching and public speaking, every address to any audience whatsoever. You can then learn from everything you hear and see which is well done. Equally, you can learn what to avoid from whatever you see or hear that is less well done. For this you need to be able to put your finger precisely on the strengths and weaknesses of each performance. To do that entails having some such battery of tests, although you do not have to use the above. It is also in my mind that if you examine every address you hear in some detail, you will then develop a sensitivity on these points which will influence your own preaching and occasional 'few words', to the noticeable benefit of your hearers.

Exercise 2. Storekeeping

One of my favourite New Testament verses is Matt. 13.52. 'Every scribe who has been trained for the Kingdom of Heaven is like a householder who brings out of his treasure what is new and what is old'. Actually, I prefer – with the support of Messrs Bauer, Arndt and Gringrich – the translation 'store' to treasure. My second recommendation to you is to keep your store well stocked. The business of the Jewish scribe was to know the 'Law' and its rabbinical interpretation. Our business as scribes of the Kingdom is with Theology in the broad sense of that term. We should be well read in Scripture, in Christian Doctrine and its sources, the criteria of Christian conduct, the forms of Christian worship and have at least an outline knowledge of the Church's history.

Seminary and or theological college training put something on our shelves. Now it is for us like the 'good and faithful servants' of the parable to make that capital grow. We must not let ourselves off by saying, 'The ordinary parishioner does not need all that deep Theology'. They may not – although it is very easy to underestimate the 'simple faithful' – but we do. The teachers in the Infants Department have completed their own primary education, their secondary education and spent at least three years in tertiary education. My tutors when I was an undergraduate were not merely graduates, but established scholars. When I preach on a subject I should not be using everything from that particular shelf in my store. I should have reserves in depth as does a schoolteacher or a university teacher. Moreover, unless my own theological thinking is alive and robust, what I offer to others will be shallow, shabby and unserviceable.

Exercise 3. Aid spotting

Nor is it sufficient that my 'store' be satisfactorily stocked with technical Theology. We must forever be asking ourselves how we can make our knowledge serve our people. How can I explain it? How can I illustrate it? How can I bring out its practical consequences? One evening I was dining with a family where there were eight children. Sometime before dinner I went into the kitchen to see if there were any simple tasks which would not be beyond my powers. I was set to carve a large melon into a dozen portions. In the centre of the melon there was a great sticky mass of seeds which I was about to throw away. My hostess stopped me. She took them from me, washed them and put them aside to dry. 'When you are a nursery teacher', she said, 'you throw nothing away'. I never learned how those seeds were to be used to promote the education of her infant pupils, but I have never forgotten her attitude of mind, ever alert for materials for her class, ever quick to spot their potential as teaching aids.

Our attitude should be the same as hers. We must be quick to spot whatever will help us to explain, illustrate and make memorable the material we preach. Christ excelled in this. He draws on everything that happened around him. sheep-rearing, planting, harvesting, viticulture, fishing, business practices and breadmaking, (why not carpentry?) So should we, sieving all that we see and hear. We should sift all that we watch on television or read in periodicals or books, both fiction and non-fiction. We should ignore nothing that happens around us and especially to us. I am not suggesting that we treat all literature and all history, other people's lives and our own, as nothing more than one large quarry meant to yield sermon material. Life and literature must be profoundly respected for themselves. The help that they can give us as preachers is quite secondary, and yet both real and valuable. So, we should be in the habit of recognising pieces of ore from which we can extract serviceable material. Having identified them, we should hold on to them. Their presence, their availability enhances the value of the academic knowledge already gathered by making it more communicable. You can never start collecting too soon, or have too large a collection. Provided, of course, you can remember where you put each item.

Exercise 4. Collecting help

At this point I want to introduce a long quotation from a correspondent:

> 'What I do before each act of worship in which I share is to invite 2–3 members of the congregation to meet with me on at least two occasions for preparation of worship and the sermon. At the first meeting we look at the prescribed Lectionary Scripture readings and reflect generally on them. I value this discussion because it really does unpack the readings and clarifies people's questions and concerns in relation to them. By the end of our meeting (1½ hours at most) we like to be clear about the dominant theme. The group then goes away to reflect further, and we return after about a week with any additional remarks, and also stories, poems, songs etc. that throw light on the theme. I use all this material to help me in my preparation for a sermon'.

I have also heard of a parish in France where each Saturday evening the clergy meet with a group of parishioners to decide the matter and the presentation of the next day's preaching. I am very envious of that Methodist minister and those French abbés. I have sometimes discussed the coming Sunday's gospel with a lay friend and always benefitted from his or her comments. What an asset to have the regular co-operation of a group practised in reflecting on the gospel in relation to their fellow parishioners and used to articulating their needs, their suggestions and their criticisms!

With Love

With that picture of systematic lay participation in the preparation of preaching my own list of precepts, recommendations and warnings draws to an end. There is one deliberate omission to be filled.

Writing of nervousness in Chapter 10 I did not quote the remark of a barrister and local councillor, later to be Lord Mayor of his city. Speaking to a gathering of my Sixth Form he said, 'The way to deal with nervousness is to love your audience'. I have saved that bonne bouche to this point because I wish to make again the point I raised in Chapter 2, where I described how I kickstarted Richard's speech to life with the dictum 'a speech is a love affair with an audience'. Preaching must always be a love affair, or if you prefer, an affair of love. The preacher preaches because he or she loves Christ, Christ's teaching, the Church which preserves that teaching and proclaims it to successive generations, and the people to whom the Church has sent him or her, perhaps just for this one occasion, to preach Christ and His message. Preaching should begin with, be sustained by and conclude with love.

Envoi

Every word of this book has in the course of its composition and revision been read, scrutinised and sometimes corrected by Miss Yvonne Davies, Community Librarian of Llanelwy Rhuddlan in the County of Clwyd. In January 1991 Yvonne, then twenty-nine years of age, ceased to work in her libraries because of a gravely deteriorating heart-lung condition which could be remedied only by a double lung transplant. Facing a waiting period of increasing disability with no guarantee that matching organs would be found in time to save her life, Yvonne said to me, 'This situation calls for courage, common sense and love'.

I have often thought since that her formula applies to other situations less poignant, including preaching. You certainly need courage to accept the responsibility of preaching. Of common sense you can never have enough as you decide on your material, your style, your exposition and your applications. And if there be no love, leave the whole business alone.

Should you then find yourself standing in the sacristy, waiting for the service to begin, your stomach churning and your mind seemingly blank, recall Yvonne's formula. Drum up what courage you have, summon all your common sense and let Eternal Love speak through you.

Epilogue

Near And Far: Twenty Days And Twenty Years

Twenty Days

A suburban householder on a visit to a much more prosperous relative seized the opportunity to consult the richer man's gardener.

'I am very disappointed with our lawn', he said. 'I have watered, cut and rolled it regularly; I have sanded it; I have put down selective weedkiller; I have pricked it all over with a fork, and it still doesn't amount to anything. What would you recommend?'

'Well', said the gardener slowly, in a voice as rough and dry as his hands, 'If you were to leave off tormenting it awhile, it might have a chance to grow'.

I am wondering whether at this point the conscientious reader feels rather like that over-tended suburban lawn. For twelve chapters I have expounded and argued; narrated and illustrated; I have advised, exhorted and warned, and you have been on the receiving end! I have deliberately led you, sometimes in much detail, through every aspect of the preacher's art known to me. Suppose you are the Hesitant Homilist due to deliver your first sermon on the Feast of Corpus Christi in three weeks time. How can you possibly bring to bear all that I have said? In Chapter 12 there is that list of criteria for judging an address. Should you try to keep all its forty-odd questions in mind throughout the next three weeks? Or should you listen to that gardener, put all my precepts aside and follow your own instincts?

With three weeks to go, I would strip my advice down to the following principles:

1. Think all the time, 'I am going to speak to those people about the sacrament of the Eucharist'. Stress 'speak', and you are in less danger of turning up with an essay to read and more likely to have prepared something suitable for speaking out loud. Linger on the words 'to those people' so that the thought of your congregation influences every choice of matter, style and delivery.

2. Be economical. Keep your material spare, your skeleton or structure short and uncomplicated and then flesh it out quite lightly with explanations, illustrations etc. And DON'T ADD. Resist the thoughts: 'I must say something about . . . I ought to answer the objection that . . . I must work in that excellent quotation from . . . There is that story of what the little girl said at the First Communion Class'.

Recently a member of Her Majesty's Opposition told the story of his worst Parliamentary failure. It fell to him to lead the attack on the Government when it was suffering from a bad split in its own ranks, and from a suspicion of rather grave 'dirty tricks', along with a great deal of adverse media comment. Relishing the opportunity, he prepared a pungent exposé of the Government's blunders and misdeeds. On the day of the debate he unexpectedly found himself with an hour to spare before he was due to speak, and so took the opportunity to put some more work into his speech. Being used to putting words together at high speed, he was able to incorporate a good deal of new matter and to make quite a lot of alterations.

The debate began and he rose to launch this devastating verbal onslaught on a plainly apprehensive Front Bench. After a few sentences he noticed that his opponents were becoming less uneasy. He ploughed on, watching their relief becoming more and more obvious. At this point it dawned on him that his carefully prepared speech was falling flat. In that

154 The Practical Preacher

extra hour he had destroyed its effectiveness. His additions had not reinforced his arguments, but obscured them. His alterations had not honed the speech's cutting edge. They had only blunted it. With those eleventh hour 'improvements' he had not only ruined a good speech, he had thrown away the political opportunity of a lifetime.

Is the moral of my story that you should never make changes as the delivery date of your sermon draws close? Not exactly. Certainly you can substitute a better example or a more telling phrase. But be certain that it is better. A different example or phrase is not necessarily a better one. Still more important: if you put something in, take something out. If your substitute phrase or example is shorter so much the better. Changes at a late stage should shorten never lengthen.

3. Clarify. During this 'run up' period your 'theme sentence'(Chapters 5 and 6) becomes very important. Have it absolutely clear and never lose sight of it. Then get the skeleton or structure of your homily equally clear. Next, make sure of your transitions so that you can pass smoothly from one point to the next. By 'smoothly' I do not imply rapidly. At your transitions you should make a longer pause than anywhere else. You must 'paragraph'. (Chapter 9)

4. Practice your voice. You are going to SPEAK to that congregation, so practise speaking. Do it in a large room if one is available, speaking loudly and clearly and slowly, putting in what expression you can. If you know that you will have reliable amplification still practise speaking with well-filled lungs and make sure of your enunciation. Drill yourself to remember that you must be heard, that each word must be heard distinctly and without effort by anyone with normal hearing.

To summarise:

1. Think, 'I am going to speak to these people'. So:
    (a) Prepare an address to be SPOKEN.
    (b) Let the thought of the congregation influence every decision.

2. Be Economical:
   (a) Have a simple outline lightly fleshed.
   (b) Do not, as time gets shorter, add anything ...
       You can make a change if it is an undoubted
       improvement and certainly no longer.
3. Get Quite Clear:
   (a) Your Theme Sentence.
   (b) The Outline of your address.
   (c) The Transitions.
   (d) Think, 'I must PARAGRAPH'.
4. Practise your voice. Convince yourself, 'All this must be
   HEARD'. Then the day after Corpus Christi, you can go
   back to studying that list of forty-something questions.

Twenty years on

In those days following the first sermon the thoughts of the
neo-Homilist might wander down the following path:
   'Next Corpus Christi, in whatever church I find myself, I
could use that sermon again. The following year, even if I am
in the same church, it could serve again with a few minor
changes of presentation. And after that I may need a new one
completely. Some ministers stay in the same parish for years.
Can I go on finding new things to say about the Eucharist?
And it isn't just Corpus Christi, but the whole liturgical cycle
of Advent, Christmas, the Epiphany etc. which comes round
remorselessly year by year. Can I go on coming up with new
material or at least new ways of presenting the basic doctrines
involved?'
   Here I may take you by surprise by stating that in all
honesty my difficulty has at times been precisely the opposite
one. For instance, at one period I used to preach in the school
where I was a full-time teacher, and also two or three times a
term in the local University Chaplaincy, together with the
occasional sermon in local parishes and to Catholic
organisations. Each of these sermons was conscientiously
prepared and those given at the Chaplaincy, which were on
the long side, were very carefully worked out. It struck me one
day that within a few weeks of delivering any sermon I could
recall very little of what I had said. How wasteful, I thought,

to have spent all that time and effort and to have used the product only once!

My solution was to buy a large, stiff-backed notebook in which to keep a record of all my homilies. The next sermon I preached was in a school at a 'Parents and Families Mass'. I do remember that I spoke about the virtue of patience, a subject relevant both to parents and teachers. Afterwards I carefully entered the outline of my address in my fine new logbook. It was the last thing I wrote there. One was always too busy meeting the urgent needs of today and tomorrow to keep records of something already done and out of the way. So, there is one way to avoid repeating yourself year by year: throw away your notes, if any; forget what you have said and put yourself in the position where you always have to start again.

Perhaps that is too drastic a solution. A record of past sermons could help you to avoid repeating yourself if you check what you intend to say against last year's entry. Also, what you have said once is not to be regarded as entirely useless ever afterward. If what you have said before helped people, then it may very well help them to hear it once again, but with some variations both of material and presentation. We should never lose sight of Matthew's dictum about the scribe of the Kingdom who 'brings out of his store what is new and what is old'.

I should like to refine that principle somewhat: Bring out the old, but let it never be stale and tired; bring out the new, but do not let it be raw and unassimilable, like that patch of raw, unshrunk cloth which tore the rest of the fabric. At the end of the building in which I write there is an oak tree planted in 1849 by a visiting Jesuit General. It is undoubtedly old, but there is nothing stale about it. It is literally rooted in the past, but it is a living force reaching upward (it overtops our four-storey tower) and outward (it had recently to be lopped for the sake of the building and the surrounding trees). Every year it extends its branches with new shoots and puts out fresh foliage. The new shoots will not change the characteristic upthrusting silhouette, but only extend it. Nor will the tender young leaves seem out of place against the rough, weather-worn bark of the trunk.

The mind of the preacher should be alive and growing, rather like a healthy oak. That was not the formula of some priests of my generation. They took it that their seminary training had kitted them out for the rest of their lives. They would take what they had learned there about God and humanity (they would say 'man') and serve up pieces of it to their flocks, using the same formulae and probably the same examples which they had quoted in their exams. They would administer the sacraments in the age-old way and lead people in the same devotional practices, until the day when they were buried with the same rites which they had used when they took their first funeral. In this way they would preserve the faith, the morals, the sacraments and the piety of themselves and their people. Unfortunately for themselves - and their people - they were resisting life itself. They were trying to make themselves into machines, for it is a machine which goes on operating in exactly the same way, turning out precisely the same product until it wears out.

Predictably, the world changed around them, a fact with which they refused to be reconciled. Phrases such as 'modern education', 'young people nowadays' and 'the world today' were on their lips always terms of condemnation. Then the Church itself, being a living entity, threw off the efforts of such people to fossilise it. Theologians broke new ground as worthwhile theologians have always done. Scripture scholars shed new light on Holy Writ. Liturgical studies greatly altered our understanding of our forms of worship. There was a growing appreciation of the discoveries of psychologists, sociologists and educationalists, together with a realisation that these new insights needed to be assimilated into the pastoral work of the Church. King Canute is said to have installed himself on the beach and regally forbidden the tide to come in. Of course, it came, and the King splashed his way back with rather less dignity to the other side of the highwater mark. Where, with the tide of change swirling through the Church itself, could the clerical Canutes go? They could only take refuge in their memories, their nostalgia and their disapproval, looking for support to other flood victims, clerical and lay. It was a sad thing to watch, sometimes pathetic, often exasperating, occasionally approaching the dignity of tragedy.

A minister of religion serves a living people in the living body of the Church. We should be offering them living truth, living wisdom, living inspiration. So, let your mind, and with it your imagination and your heart, grow like a tree. Let it reach downward into the past, rooting itself in the traditions and classics of the Church. Let it reach outwards with contemporary scholars in their explorations, but always with discretion.

Never try to prove that you are today's person by clutching at the newest theory, adopting the latest jargon and running after whatever is, to use a phrase from this month's 'Tatler', 'desperately in'. Be ready to learn from the past and the moderns, accepting neither wholly uncritically. Both the people of the past and the writers of the present have much to teach us and both can at times mislead. Read always with discernment for you are responsible not only for what your own mind absorbs, but also for what you are going to offer your people.

A tree extracts nutrients not only from the soil, but draws upon the atmosphere and even the light. We should nourish ourselves from the world around us, from observing people and talking to them, and especially listening to them. Too many of us think it our business only to hand out wisdom and knowledge. We listen merely to diagnose and prescribe. One of the most educative remarks I ever heard was spoken by my Headmaster, 'There is no-one', he said, 'who can't teach you something'. At the time I was not a pupil, but his deputy, and the better able to appreciate the truth of his dictum. It crystallized for me a principle which I had to some extent been following for years, but which I had never formulated for myself.

By now my neo-Homilist may feel both baffled and exasperated. The difficulty was precise and severely practical, 'How in twenty years time do I avoid preaching substantially the same sermon year by year?' My answer has been to discourse widely and at length on the continuous self-education of the minister. That is the answer, and it is as down to earth and as practical as the query. So, read and think; observe and reflect; listen and learn. Do these things receptively and sympathetically, opening not only your mind, but also your imagination and your heart. Also do them responsibly, sifting everything that comes to you by these various routes, keeping only what may prove genuinely nutritious for you and your congregation.

In Chapter 4 I wrote, 'Were you to ask a good experienced teacher to address the First Form and the Sixth about the same subject and in exactly the same words, I doubt if he or she could do it. They would automatically adapt their approach and their vocabulary to the class'. Follow the advice given in the previous paragraphs, even if you can only do it spasmodically, and I promise that you will find yourself unable to say the same thing year after year even when speaking on the same subject to the same audience. Your understanding of the subject and your view of how it is relevant to your congregation will both have developed. You will be a living, developing person, your preaching alive and developing with you.

Long live the Preacher! A Practical Preacher, of course.